Environmental Economics

D1569590

Environmental Economics

A Critique of Benefit-Cost Analysis

Philip E. Graves

ROWMAN & LITTLEFIELD PUBLISHERS, INC.
Lanham • Boulder • New York • Toronto • Plymouth, UK

ROWMAN & LITTLEFIELD PUBLISHERS, INC.

Published in the United States of America
by Rowman & Littlefield Publishers, Inc.
A wholly owned subsidary of The Rowman & Littlefield Publishing Group, Inc.
4501 Forbes Boulevard, Suite 200, Lanham, Maryland 20706
www.rowmanlittlefield.com

Estover Road, Plymouth PL6 7PY, United Kingdom

British Library Cataloguing in Publication Information Available

Library of Congress Cataloging-in-Publication Data
Graves, Philip E.
  Environmental economics : a critique of benefit-cost analysis / Philip Graves.
    p. cm.
  Includes bibliographical references and index.
  ISBN-13: 978-0-7425-4698-1 (cloth : alk. paper)
  ISBN-10: 0-7425-4698-5 (cloth : alk. paper)
  ISBN-13: 978-0-7425-4699-8 (pbk.)
  ISBN-10: 0-7425-4699-3 (pbk. : alk. paper)
  1. Environmental economics. I. Title.
  HC79.E5G686 2007
  333.7—dc22

                                                                2006100583

Printed in the United States of America

Dedicated to Jessica and Wendy

Contents

Acknowledgments

I would like to acknowledge George S. Tolley at the University of Chicago for many conversations over many years. Without George's knowledge and insights, this book could not have been written. I would also like to acknowledge Amit Batabyal, Charles de Bartolome, Kristi Chapin, Nick Flores, Wolfgang Keller, Jim Markusen, Anna Rubinchik-Pessach, Kerry Smith, Randy Walsh, Stephan Weiler, and Jeff Zax for comments on several occasions. I am additionally grateful for numerous seminar/workshop comments on the material in chapter 8 at the University of British Columbia Law School, University of Chicago, University of Colorado, Colorado State University, George Mason University, Georgia State University, University of Missouri, North Carolina State University, Rochester Institute of Technology, West Virginia University, and the University of Wyoming. Also, I wish to thank Brian Romer at Roman & Littlefield for encouragement from inception to final product, and Bridgette Moore for her careful work in bringing this book to fruition.

I

ECONOMICS BACKGROUND— WHY ECONOMISTS LIKE BENEFIT-COST ANALYSIS

Environmentalists are often mystified as to why economists are so enamored with the market system. Indeed, *environmental economics* is seen by many people to be an oxymoron, like jumbo shrimp or plastic silverware. Markets appear to be so steeped in greed, with success and failure being measured in dollars, as to seem largely irrelevant to the loftier goals of those concerned with the environment. Yet, in part I, the case is made that the *logic* of the market is not only sensible but has relevance, possibly great relevance, to appropriate environmental decisions.

In economics, everything revolves around the choices imposed on us by scarcity. Because we cannot have everything we want, trade-offs are inevitable. Economists believe that if we think hard about those trade-offs (using benefit-cost analysis, when markets are not available) that we will make better decisions than if we do not. It is argued that in the extreme case of perfect information, thinking about the benefits and costs should lead to "perfect" decisions; if we had either more or less environmental quality, we would be worse off. Even among economists, however, there is spirited debate about whether we do the calculations at all right (indeed, the principal claim of this book is that we do the calculations horribly wrong, with a systematic bias against environmental quality).

Yes, environmentalists and other ethicists find much to criticize about the economists' way of thinking. The human-centered approach—the greed, the dollars—are seen by many as just the tip of the iceberg of problems with the approach of the economist. Relying exclusively on human preferences is argued by environmentalists to be inappropriate for a variety of reasons; other things matter. It could be argued, as one example, that we have flawed preferences, enjoying too many goods that involve excessive pollution in

1

their production or consumption. Or we might just be too ignorant to know meaningfully the long-term consequences of our actions—perhaps destroying ourselves, after we have destroyed everything else.

Both the views of economists (scarcity matters) and the views of environmentalists and philosophers (other things matter, too) have merit. The broad range of activities the latter groups might ideally like to pursue does not, however, provide much specific practical guidance about what to do now with the limited resources we have available. How do we decide, for example, whether to devote scarce resources to preserve and improve the ocean's reefs or to reduce carbon dioxide (CO_2) buildup? Save a whale species or reduce tropical deforestation? Clean the air or clean the water? And just as important, we also have to decide *how much* of such things to do. The list of desirable environmental actions to be taken is virtually unlimited, while the resources that will realistically be allocated toward them are quite limited. We must *decide*.

So, most economists, even those who are quite skeptical about the accuracy of benefit-cost analyses, believe economic tools are useful in prioritizing the many projects that environmentalists advance, identifying the "more important" things to do first (a principal point of Lomborg).[1] If some projects appear to have costs ten times the benefits and others have benefits ten times the costs, both environmentalists and economists would be likely to agree that we should pursue the latter before turning to the former—even if measurement problems make most of the numbers in all projects dubious.

Chapter 1 considers basic matters of logic and philosophy, arguing that scarcity implies that decisions have to be made. Good decisions have advantages greater than disadvantages. Advantages, when measured with dollar units, are called the *benefits* of the decision. Disadvantages, when measured with dollar units, are called the *costs* of the decision. Chapter 1 sets the stage for the discussion in chapter 2 of why economists like the prices and quantities—for ordinary non-environmental goods—that emerge from voluntary interactions among suppliers and demanders in private markets. This chapter also reveals an important parallel between the optimal provision of ordinary goods and the optimal provision of environmental goods under ideal conditions.

In introductory principles of microeconomics courses, the supply-and-demand discussions typically make little reference to the role of time in economic decisions. Yet, many projects (both environmental and non-environmental) involve benefits and costs that occur over lengthy periods. And the time patterns of benefits and costs can be quite different for different projects, though we can generally get no benefits at all until at least some costs have first been incurred. Some projects will involve benefits that largely occur in the distant future while others have benefits occurring much more immediately. Yet, we have to decide *now* which to pursue among such projects. Chapter 3 clarifies the role of discounting in the benefit-cost analysis of long-term projects.

The material in chapters 1, 2, and 3 provides what one might call an optimistic base-case scenario. That is, *if* the knowledge of the benefits and costs of environmental goods were as accurately measured as it is for ordinary private goods, our decisions would lead us to the proper relative amounts of all goods—both ordinary and environmental—at each point in time.

This is not to say that environmentalists would necessarily agree with the preceding, for reasons discussed in depth. But there would be far less disagreement under such ideal circumstances. The remaining chapters in the book (contained in parts II, III, IV, and V) will clarify why the economic evaluations result in systematic underprovision, possibly severe underprovision, of environmental goods.

The reader might well ask "Why present the optimistic base-case scenario of chapters 1, 2, and 3 at all, if it is to be later systematically undermined?" The answer is best seen by analogy to the auto repairman. The repairman cannot begin to diagnose what is wrong with a poorly functioning car without knowing how cars were designed to work when they work perfectly. So we shall first study the "perfect market" to better understand its many imperfections in successive chapters.

NOTE

1. Bjørn Lomborg, *The Skeptical Environmentalist: Measuring the Real State of the World* (Cambridge: Cambridge University Press, 2001).

1

Introductory Matters of Logic and Philosophy

It would be wonderful if we all could have everything we want . . . large homes, fast cars, great food—all of the "toys"—but also a beautiful, pristine environment in which to enjoy our riches. Unfortunately, this is not the world we live in. We live in a world characterized by *scarcity*. By scarcity, an economist merely means that we have wants for goods and services that are relatively greater than the resources available to fully satisfy those wants. Scarcity, in this important sense, will always be with us, because we appear to have a lot of imagination about things we might like (poverty, defined as any fixed living standard, need not be ever-present, though).

Because we cannot have everything we want, we have to choose among the available goods, ideally buying those that give us the most satisfaction given our income. But, should environmental goods be thought about so crassly? Should they be merely a matter of choice or is there a moral or ethical imperative to "do the right thing"?

Figure 1.1 provides a number of insights into the preceding issues.

The existence of the curved production possibilities frontier, labeled PPF, in this figure represents the fact of scarcity at a point in time. The position of the curve, for a population of a given size, indicates how severe the impact of scarcity is—for the same population size, a PPF curve far to the northeast represents a rich society, with abundant quantities of either or both environmental and non-environmental goods, relative to a PPF near the origin. This curve has been shifting out, at least since the Industrial Revolution, *allowing* more of both types of goods over time.[1]

But, at any given time, we can only obtain combinations of ordinary and environmental goods that lie on, or inside, the PPF curve—we cannot achieve points, like D, that lie to the northeast of the PPF curve. However,

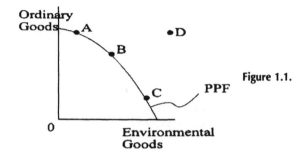

Figure 1.1.

because both ordinary goods and environmental goods give us satisfaction, we would not want to be at any point inside the production possibilities frontier. So, because points outside the PPF are not feasible and points inside the PPF are not desirable, we want to choose among points, such as A or B or C, that lie on the PPF. But where? Which point do we want?

The ardent environmentalist might argue that we have a moral or ethical imperative to maximize environmental quality, perhaps at a point such as C, with high environmental quality but not many ordinary private goods. The hedonistic consumer might argue for a point, such as A, with relatively many ordinary goods, consumed in a somewhat dirty environment with a good deal of ecological damage occurring. We *have* to make a choice, and doing nothing is just another choice.

If it were possible to sell environmental goods in ordinary markets like an ordinary good, the market would provide a solution (one among many, but one with some desirable properties) to the problem of how much of each good to provide, as we shall see in greater detail in the next two chapters. But we are not able to buy clean air like we do a six-pack of cola . . . is it even appropriate to think this way? That the dollars themselves mean nothing should be clear from figure 1.1—we are faced with trade-offs between real physical goods of two types, both of which are desirable. The use of dollars will be seen to actually obscure what is happening in the economic system; they are merely units of account.

In some respects, it does not matter whether environmentalists feel that the economists' way of thinking about how to allocate our scarce resources is right or wrong. A far-reaching ruling published by the Federal Register in 1981 now *requires* that benefit-cost analysis be used for all significant federal regulatory actions. If environmentalists are unwilling to play within the rules of the game they will be ignored in the policy arena, and the rules of the game are benefit-cost analysis. However, deeply held moral and ethical beliefs about the environment often do, and should, inform policy choices, because they affect environmental demands if measurement problems can be overcome, which is a topic of much of this book.

Returning to figure 1.1, it is clear that we would not want a zero pollution economy, with maximal environmental quality—a zero pollution economy is an economy with zero production of ordinary goods, hence a zero population economy. The costs of having a zero human environmental impact would exceed the benefits even to environmentalists, because they would no longer exist.

But attempting to maximize the amount of ordinary goods would similarly have costs greater than benefits—uncontrolled pollution is clearly too much, particularly for rich countries with abundant ordinary goods and high environmental demands. But where should we go between these extremes? What sort of balance should we attempt to strike between the ordinary goods that we want and the environmental quality that we also want?

The environmentalist might wonder what gives humans the right to decide. But there exists no other species *to* decide so humans are, inevitably, the decision makers. The concept of a good environment vis-à-vis a bad environment is inherently human. . . . Mother Nature is mute on the issue. Natural environments have fluctuated wildly in terms of atmospheric chemistry, temperature, species composition, and so on. Indeed, some of the most highly manicured artificial environments imaginable, Japanese koi gardens are felt by many to be beautiful environments.

One might argue, as an operating principle, that it is environmental *change* that is to be avoided, specifically environmental changes associated with human activity. Yet change is also a pervasive and integral part of the natural order. To attempt to prevent all environmental change would interfere with complex evolving dynamic processes about which we know little.

Illustrating, evidence is cumulating that human activity is at least a partial cause of observed global warming. But it is also the case that global temperature changes have occurred with great regularity throughout the existence of Earth. In the quite recent past, humans were concerned about global *cooling*, not global warming. One might well imagine a situation in which increasing greenhouse gas emissions would be seen by humans as a *desirable* by-product of the industrial age, preventing an ice age that might otherwise have occurred. Should we, in our efforts to avoid environmental changes associated with our activities, cease producing our vast array of enjoyable products, so that an ice age that is natural (but would make humans miserable worldwide) can happen?

One tends to feel more sympathy for species (e.g., the dinosaurs) if they are wiped out by external changes in their environment (e.g., a comet striking the Yucatan peninsula) than if they were wiped out in other ways (e.g., the rise of mammals). Yet both events are in every meaningful sense natural—Mother Nature does not "care." But, we humans *do* care—our species is the first to be concerned about environmental quality and our impact on environmental quality.[2] At a minimum we would all like to avoid or at least postpone as long as possible, for humans, the ultimate fate of all species (extinction), particularly if that eventual destruction is brought about by our own activities. But we also want to do more than this, because we care not just about humans but also about the myriad of species that make up local, regional, and global ecosystems.

With the preceding discussion in mind, the following assertions will be in place for the rest of the book:

- We cannot have all of the things—environmental and non-environmental—that we want.
- We—humans—therefore face inevitable trade-offs between environmental and non-environmental goods. We must choose, and even doing nothing is itself a choice.[3]
- We want to make wise choices.

But, what are wise choices? How do we decide what is a good thing to do and what is not? Much of the rest of this book is about the problems that, taken together, lead us to *think* we are making wise choices when we are not. The primary reason we make unwise choices is that we lack *perfect information* about all the consequences of the choice at the time the choice is made. All of us have bought some ordinary item, clothes or some gadget, only to realize quickly thereafter that the purchase was a mistake. We would never have bought the item if we had perfect information beforehand about the consequences of its purchase.

What kind of perfect knowledge do we need to make perfect decisions? Do we need to know about the existence or nonexistence of a deity or about what happens inside the black holes of physics? No. What we need to know is much easier to know, at least for ordinary private goods. What we need to know at any point in time are *tastes, technology,* and *prices.*

Considering first demanders, you cannot make informed decisions about whether to buy something unless you know how much you like it (tastes, sometimes called preferences) and how much it costs relative to other goods (prices). For example, some people do not buy steak because they do not like it, and others might not buy it because it is expensive, despite liking it quite a lot. Similarly, others *do* buy steak, despite thinking it too expensive, because they like it a great deal, and others will buy the steak because it seems inexpensive to them at their income level.

We will return in the next chapter to a discussion of the role played by income, and fairness more generally, in demands for non-environmental (and environmental) goods. For now, if consumers know their tastes and the prices of available goods, they will make what *for them* will be rational decisions, that is, decisions that make them as well off as possible.[4] They will buy, given their tastes, goods if the benefits they perceive, expressed in dollar terms, exceed the price they must pay (that price will, in turn, represent how much of *other* goods they could have had—the dollars themselves, as always, mean nothing).

For suppliers, you cannot know whether you wish to produce and sell a good unless you know how to produce the good (technology) as well as input and output prices. To clarify, suppose you know all of the combinations of inputs that can produce any quantity of the good. Some combinations might be labor intensive (e.g., many people cutting and sewing ties by hand), and others might be quite capital intensive (e.g., a few people running large machines that cut and sew the ties). If labor is abundant and hence inexpensive, you might be able to produce a given number of ties most cheaply with the first technology, but if labor is expensive and capital is relatively cheap, you might be better off with the second technology. There can be no best technology, from your standpoint, until you know the relative prices of labor and capital (and other inputs, in general, such as materials and energy).

When you have picked your best technology, which depends on relative input prices as just discussed, you will want to produce any good that adds more to your revenue than it adds to your costs, because that will make you better off.

The economic way of thinking described previously is actually the same in essential respects whether you are a supplier or a demander—any individual decision, whether you are buying or selling, involves both benefits and costs. Some decisions are *discrete*, being in the nature of all-or-nothing choices (e.g., going to college, getting married, buying a house [consumers] or opening or closing a business [producers]). In the environmental setting, an example of a discrete decision would be to save a species from extinction—it is either saved or not. The rational decision maker will opt for a discrete choice any time the total benefits of the choice exceed the total costs of the choice, for example, going to college if it is felt that the income and social benefits exceed the (considerable) costs.

But most important decisions we make are *continuous*, being of the a-little-more-or-less rather than of the all-or-nothing type. Ordinary examples would be how much to study one course relative to another, how much to study relative to partying, or how many pizza slices to consume in an evening. Environmental examples might be how much to clean the air or water. For such decisions, it is *marginal* benefits and *marginal* costs that matter—the first hour of study matters more than the last, as does the first pizza slice. Indeed, it is generally the case that when we have small quantities of any good, additional amounts are worth more to us than if we had large quantities of the good. Small amounts of potable water, say in a desert, are extremely valuable, but that value falls rapidly as we get more.

Similarly, what we give up (the marginal cost) to get additional quantities tends to become larger the more of any activity we pursue. The cost of an extra hour studying a particular course, say economics, is not high if you are only studying a little. But as you study more economics, what you are giving up (study on other subjects or leisure) is becoming more valuable.

The preceding discussion can be greatly clarified with reference to figure 1.2, which for present purposes is intended to apply only at the individual level—some consumer or producer making a decision about how much to do of some activity. Literally any activity, A, affecting an individual's welfare could be on the x-axis; but for concreteness, let's assume it is studying environmental economics (it could be slices of pizza eaten, hours of exercise, or cars produced).

The case of discrete choice is actually subsumed in this case—the decision to engage in any of the activity at all. This follows from the fact that at *very* low levels of economic study the benefits almost certainly are greater than the costs. To not study at all means that an F is coming (in the case of the activity of consuming water, death would be coming). So, the more interesting question is how much study should an individual engage in? A rational student would want to add to his or her hours of study as long as he or she was made better off by doing so (remember, he or she is the decision maker, not anyone else, including parents).

Referring to figure 1.2, we want to study (or eat pizza slices or exercise or produce cars) as long as the added gains from study (the *marginal benefits*, in the jargon of economists) are greater than the added losses from study (the *marginal costs*). This occurs at study effort level A* in figure 1.2. Notice, critically, that while one can do too little of a good activity, one can also do too much. At $A_{too\ little}$ we are failing to make ourselves as well off as possible, losing net benefits depicted by area DBG. But, even though *I* think you should always study more (but remember I am not the decision maker), at $A_{too\ much}$ the last hour studied has costs—to you—far in excess of benefits; perhaps at such a high study effort on economics, you are learning material beyond that necessary to get an A and you are flunking another course. The lesson here is that, even for good things, such as study (or environmental quality), one can have either too much or too little.

The problem gets considerably more complicated when we go from the single decision maker of figure 1.2 to a world of many decision makers. This is, in fact, the biggest single difference between markets for ordinary private goods, where individuals can purchase what they *individually* want and markets for public goods. For public goods, such as environmental quality, we are attempting to determine how much of something we should provide when everyone receives that quantity.

It turns out that no matter what level of public goods we supply we are confronted with clashes of values in a way that is not present for ordinary private goods. To clarify, if Alan is a vegetarian who likes tofu burgers (private goods), he enters the tofu burger market and buys what he wants. Betty, a carnivore, enters the hamburger market and buys what she wants. There is

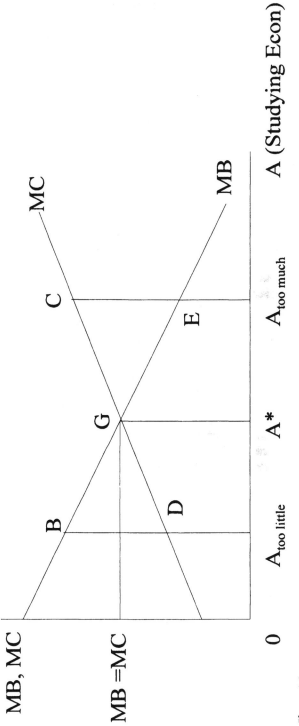

Figure 1.2.

no clash of values in the sense that *both* Alan and Betty can get what they want. There is much more social strife regarding the chosen amount of, say, air quality, because the selected amount is unlikely to be *individually* optimal for either Alan or Betty. In fact, hardly anyone will be *exactly* pleased with the chosen air quality—many people, given the costs of provision, will want much lower quality (the poor, the healthy, and those generally who prefer ordinary goods), and others will want much higher quality (the rich, the sick, and those not caring much for ordinary goods). Yet we have to have *some* air quality, hence the clashes of values. We will return to this problem in detail in chapter 5.

Foreshadowing, one might reasonably argue that in many environmental cases we know next to nothing about the location of the (necessarily aggregated) marginal benefit and marginal cost curves of figure 1.2. If benefits are actually twice what we think they are, we will undersupply environmental quality. Indeed, one might argue that we know so little about where those marginal benefit and the marginal cost curves are that even attempting to make rational choices is a ludicrous activity (this roughly characterizes Ackerman and Heinzerling's argument).[5]

Indeed in Europe many environmental decisions are made, not according to benefit-cost analysis, but according to something called the "Precautionary Principle." This principle argues that if we are not *very* certain about the full implications of human decisions, we should err on the side of caution, regardless of measured costs and benefits. After completing this book, it is likely that you will find the Precautionary Principle to be an appealing interim strategy, at least until we do a *much* better job of measuring environmental benefits.

In a similar vein, one might argue that political problems (e.g., political action committee [PAC] contributions from deep-pocket polluters in the United States or similar special interest arrangements throughout the world) result in irrational relative amounts of various environmental and non-environmental goods. We shall come back to this topic in detail in the closing discussion. It should be noted at the outset, however, that optimal environmental quality is not a Republican, conservative, Democrat, or liberal issue. The relative amount of environmental and non-environmental goods to produce is a resource allocation issue, and while there may be systematic differences in Republican and Democrat (or Tory and Labour) attitudes, it is not entirely clear that this is so. One sees hedonistic Democrats and environmentalist Republicans. Moreover, policies that environmentalists would view as good have occurred under both major parties (e.g., Richard Nixon and the Clean Air Act); similarly, bad policies have occurred under both major parties.

For now, however, we are focusing on perfectly functioning markets for ordinary goods, where it is transparently clear that we must make *individual* choices; they are unavoidable. While it is also true that choices are unavoidable for environmental and other public goods, the fact that such choices are no longer individual, but rather collective, adds great complexity. Along with that complexity comes great potential for bad decisions. The goal of this book is to increase the likelihood of making *better* choices, by clarifying in great detail why bad choices get made.

In the next chapter we will see in detail how the market economy operates in an ideal situation, a situation with no missing markets. Why economists like the market outcome for ordinary goods under these ideal circumstances will also be clarified. Looking more carefully at those ideal circumstances, economists often say that environmental problems stem from market failure. We shall see that a better characterization would be to argue that environmental problems stem from a failure to have markets. This leads to a useful parallel between ordinary goods and environmental goods. *If* we could provide environmental goods at the same levels a *perfectly functioning* private market would—if such a market could exist—we would have the desired relative amounts of goods of all types. Unfortunately, as the bulk of this book will establish, this is an elusive goal as a practical matter . . . but on to perfectly functioning markets!

QUESTIONS FOR DISCUSSION

1. Should nonhuman values play a role in environmental policy decisions? (Should the cow have a say in how much steak gets produced?) How can we know the magnitude of nonhuman preferences? Does it matter whether the species has limited cognitive ability (e.g., the cow) or does not (e.g., the tree)? When would we be guilty of *speciesism* (favoring some species and disfavoring others)?

2. Many environmentalists favor reintroduction of species, say wolves, in certain locations . . . but how do we decide how many wolves to introduce?

3. Should there be preferences over preferences—are some preferences better than others? If so, how do we decide whose preferences are best? (This important topic will be revisited in discussion after chapter 2, as it is of great philosophical interest.)

4. Marginal benefits and marginal costs are *subjective*, varying with each individual. For ordinary private goods, this is not a problem, because we can all decide individually—if you like broccoli you buy lots of it relative to asparagus and vice versa for those who prefer asparagus. Why is the subjectivity of preferences a problem for environmental goods?

5. Marginal costs of ordinary goods are lower for rich people (who have to give up less important goods to acquire more of something) than for poor people (who have higher value alternative uses for their

resources). Is this fair? Is it fair, in figure 1.2, for two people who study the same amount to get different grades because one is more innately intelligent? Discuss why you think one case might be unfair while the other might be fair? Hint: While there is no definitive answer to these questions, in many settings, it is the rules of the game that must be determined to be fair or unfair; once the rules are agreed on and followed diligently, outcomes often are no longer viewed as unfair. Consider horse races and notions of equality of outcome versus equality of opportunity. (Again, the importance of this issue will require that we return to it.)

6. Suppose you do not a) pay all of the marginal costs of some activity or b) receive all of the marginal benefits of some activity. Will your decision about how much of that activity to engage in still be correct from your perspective? From society's perspective?

NOTES

1. At very low levels of income and population, we would have had—without needing to devote any of our scarce resources to its production—large amounts of environmental quality. The human concern in such an era would merely be with ordinary goods, with say shelter on one axis and food on the other in figure 1.1. This era is of limited relevance to the modern world, whether developed or developing, with large—and growing—population and income.

2. Were we around sixty-five million years ago with our current incomes and environmental sensibilities, it is quite likely that we would have attempted to save the dinosaurs in climate-controlled zoos. There would, of course, later come to be a vocal minority—perhaps even a majority—of people arguing for the release of velociraptors and the like back into their natural settings, despite the problems that would likely ensue.

3. Environmentalists sometimes argue that there is no choice regarding environmental goods, that there are moral imperatives analogous to the Ten Commandments. But, consider the most obvious of those, "Thou shall not kill." Suppose you are a teenager coming home late one night, being quiet so as not wake your parents. Just as you are passing the family shotgun in the hallway, you hear the voice of an intruder saying to your parents "Now that you've seen my face, I have to kill you because I can't leave any witnesses!" The intruder does not know you're there—do you kill an unknown intruder to prevent the deaths of both your parents? To be sure, most of the time we would never *choose* to kill anyone because virtually all the time such unsavory situations are not present. Usually the high moral and other costs of killing are greater than the low benefits of killing, to use jargon from successive chapters.

4. It should perhaps be emphasized that it is the *decision maker's* tastes that matter and not those of some other person, even some other wise person. Students, for example, in allocating their scarce time and money might spend far too much of

both partying, from their parents' perspectives, yet the decisions can still be rational. Rational decisions, in other words, are not necessarily *wise* as that word is often used by parents or clergy, but they will make the decision makers as well off as possible, as they see it. While we often screw up, who among us would prefer to let others make our many decisions for us?

5. Frank Ackerman and Lisa Heinzerling, *Priceless: On Knowing the Price of Everything and the Value of Nothing* (New York: The New Press, 2004).

2

Why Economists Like Market Outcomes for Ordinary Goods

We enjoy the ordinary goods we consume for many diverse reasons. One person might buy and eat broccoli because it is healthful, despite not much liking the taste; another might consume broccoli for its delicious taste, uninterested in whether it is healthful or not. One might place a great value on a refrigerator to keep beer cold; another might value the refrigerator largely to keep ice cubes or ice cream cold; yet another might value the refrigerator because it keeps vegetables fresh.

Economists do not generally care about the psychological reasons for why people like the things they like and dislike the things they dislike.[1] In fact, economists do not usually even care much about why people consume the *levels* of various goods that they do.[2] Rather, economists tend to be interested in price elasticities and income elasticities. These esoteric-sounding terms are just particular measures of how responsive *changes* in demands or supplies are to changes in prices or income. *Why* people value the things they do has no bearing on resource allocation for ordinary goods, like broccoli or a refrigerator, as long as those tastes (preferences) are stable. If tastes are stable, that is, if you do not suddenly dislike—for whatever reason—things you used to like and vice versa, it is only relative opportunities (prices and incomes) that result in changed behavior.[3]

For environmental goods, we shall see later that the case is different—the nature of preferences actually matters, and might matter greatly, to proper resource allocation. Nearly all tastes for ordinary private goods are driven by what might be called use values—we want goods because we can *use* them. We wear clothes, live in houses, eat food, and so on . . . those are use demands, and we are willing to pay to use the goods we buy.

But there are other nonuse values that underlie human willingness to pay for certain kinds of goods, particularly for environmental goods. For example, we might want a good, not for current use, but because we want to have the option to use it, an *option* demand. Or we might, personally, not care about ever using the good, but we might want to give our offspring the chance to use the good, a *bequest* value. And we might even be willing to pay to keep goods from being used at all, a *preservation* demand. As we shall see in great detail later in the book, economists are much better at determining use values than they are at gauging how important the various nonuse values are.

With the preceding discussion lurking in the background, we turn now to why economists and many others—but not everybody—like market outcomes for ordinary private goods. The use values that characterize ordinary private goods, making us willing to pay for them, stem from their having the property of being both *rivalrous* and *excludable*. That is, consumption is rivalrous in the sense that if you are wearing the t-shirt, nobody else can be wearing it; if you eat the steak, nobody else can eat it. Similarly, for ordinary private goods, excludability means that you can keep people from consuming the good, unless they pay for it. Without excludability, it would never be profitable to supply any good—most people would just use it without paying, because that would leave them with more resources available for other things.

Because ordinary private goods are rivalrous, there must be some way to decide who gets what is produced. In the market system, those who are willing to pay the going price for a good are able to acquire it. So, the interesting question becomes, "How much would people want to buy at various prices?"

The law of demand, properly understood, is not controversial. It says merely that *at lower prices people will buy more and at higher prices people will buy less, all other things being equal.* Some people who did not buy any of a good at all at high prices will begin to buy a good as it gets less expensive, while those already buying the good will buy larger quantities at lower prices. The law of demand could be expressed in many ways (e.g., algebraically or as a table of prices and quantities), but we will find it convenient and informative to use graphs. Graphically, the relationship between price and quantity demanded is downward sloping, higher prices resulting in reduced quantities demanded (a so-called inverse relationship).

The all-other-things-being-equal caveat is important, however, in that if anything else changes (income, tastes, prices of other goods, expectations of future prices, and so on) at the same time that price changes, the negative effect of higher price on quantity demanded might be swamped by the other variable. That is, suppose that the price of constant quality cars rises, yet we observe more cars sold, rather than fewer—does this imply that people desire cars more at higher prices than at lower prices? No, it must be the case that something else has changed (probably income in this case[4]). An upward sloping relationship *is* theoretically possible—just as it is possible that unicorns exist—but like unicorns, such relationships have never been observed in properly conducted studies. That buyers prefer lower prices is hardly earthshaking—most people I have asked would love to have a Ferrari or Rolls Royce automobile if it were available for $300. So, we all would like to pay lower prices for the things we buy or might buy . . . if we could actually buy them at those lower prices. But this requires that we think about supply, because suppliers are quite unlikely to offer Ferraris and Rolls Royces for $300.

The law of supply is also straightforward. It argues that *at higher prices people will supply larger quantities, all other things being equal.* Recall that rational decision makers will be producing where marginal benefits (price for competitive suppliers) equal marginal costs to make themselves as well off as possible. Hence, with a now-higher price, the many existing suppliers will find that their marginal benefits of producing exceed marginal costs at current production levels. If producers offer a variety of products, they will want to produce relatively more of the product whose price has risen. Even if only producing the product whose price rises, it will be in their interest to increase output by hiring more variable inputs (this might involve running the machinery faster, adding shifts, overtime for workers, and so on).

As with demand, supply relationships could be depicted with algebra, tables, or graphs. The latter is most convenient, especially when we put demand and supply on the same graph for reasons that will become clear.

Most demand-and-supply curves have a time dimension. Consider some ordinary good, say steak. If you were to ask someone how much steak he or she consumes, the answer three pounds would not be meaningful. Three pounds would be a great deal of steak if that much were eaten daily but might not be abnormally high or low for weekly consumption—if the three pound answer applied to yearly consumption, he or she hardly eats steak at all. Throughout the remainder of the book, it will not matter greatly what time period is being considered, but bear in mind that *some* time period is typically implicit.[5]

To postpone problems that we will return to, particularly for environmental goods, some simplifying assumptions are made for the rest of this chapter. It is assumed that many buyers have perfect information about their tastes and the prices of the available goods and that many sellers have perfect information about production technology and the prices of both the goods they sell and the inputs hired to produce the goods. The many here means so many that no one buyer or seller and no small group in collusion can affect market price by how much they buy or sell. Moreover, though not critical, we shall assume perfect mobility of resources.[6]

Figure 2.1 shows a traditional supply-and-demand curve diagram, say for monthly consumption of steak. At a high price of $15 per pound of steak, suppliers would like to supply large quantities of steak, but people would only buy Q_{DH} at that price. If steak is, for whatever reason, relatively expensive, we will attempt to find substitutes for it, perhaps making chicken, cheese, or vegetarian dishes as alternatives. Hence, people will buy a smaller amount of steak if it becomes more expensive.

Similarly, at a low $5 per pound price of steak, people would like to buy large quantities, but not many suppliers would be willing to supply steak. At a low price of steak, some people who normally consume chicken or fish will substitute steak while other people will just increase the frequency of steak consumption during the time period. Note that for both high and low prices, it is the *lesser* of the quantity demanded or supplied that is actually exchanged—in a voluntary world, people are not required to either buy or sell more than they would like at the going price.

In our example, only at one price, $10 per pound, is what demanders want to do consistent with what suppliers want to do. This price is said to be the equilibrium price, because at any other price, forces are set in motion that cause a return to the equilibrium price. At lower prices, people want to buy more than people are willing to sell. Frustrated demanders, who cannot acquire the good at the going price, will bid more. Additionally, sellers—seeing long lines—will see that it is in their interest to raise prices.

Similarly, at prices above the equilibrium $10 per pound price, sellers will not be able to sell as much as they would like to produce—inventories

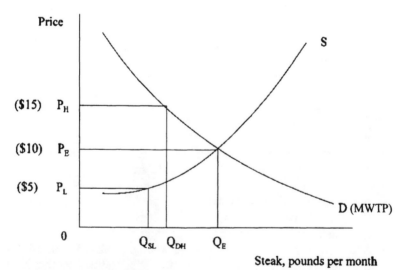

Figure 2.1. Market equilibrium

will increase and sellers will be forced to cut prices to get rid of them. Only the price that clears the market—that is consistent with what *both* buyers and sellers want to do at various prices is sustainable. Of course, it is certainly the case that buyers would like a lower price (but only if they can actually *get* the steak at that price), and sellers would like a higher price (but only if they can actually *sell* the steak at that price).[7]

The preceding is likely to be quite familiar to the reader, because the role of equilibrium price in making consistent what buyers and sellers want to do is emphasized extensively in beginning principles of microeconomics courses. This emphasis is fine for understanding how ordinary markets lead to spontaneous coordination of the behavior of buyers and sellers. But to understand why economists actually *like* the market outcome, more needs to be explained.

Figure 2.1 considered market outcomes from the perspective of the price that makes what sellers want to do consistent with what buyers want to do, the price that clears the market. Figure 2.2 looks at the steak market in a different way, focusing on the horizontal axis.[8]

A first noteworthy thing about figure 2.2 is that dollars are merely units of account, with no moral or ethical significance; they actually obscure the trade-offs we necessarily face. As discussed in chapter 1, if we have a small amount of anything (e.g., water when thirsty) it is worth a lot, in terms of giving up other goods that we also care about. If, on the other hand, we have large amounts of a good, it is worth little. How much we are willing to pay just reflects how much we already have of various goods—if we have little we are willing to pay more than if we have much.

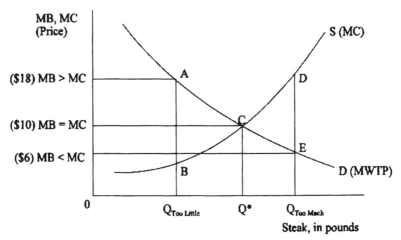

Figure 2.2.   Efficiency of market outcomes

Thus, the demand curve in figure 2.2 is also labeled MWTP for marginal willingness to pay. This just reflects the fact that, at lower prices, we will substitute more of the now-cheaper good for other, more expensive, goods. If there are no good substitutes for a good, purchases will not fall much with rising prices (the demand curve will be relatively steep). If there are many good substitutes for a good, dramatic reductions in quantity demanded occur with price rises (the demand curve will be relatively flat). Ultimately, how people react to changing prices stems from self-interest; we want to get the best bundle of goods we can with the income we have, shifting from goods that rise in price to those that fall in price as long as that can make us better off.

On the supply side, some suppliers are good at producing any particular good and would be willing to supply at fairly low prices. As long as a supplier's added cost is less than the added revenue (price in competitive markets[9]) received, the supplier will want to supply the good (hence the label of MC for marginal cost in parentheses on the supply curve in figure 2.2). As with the consumer, this, too, follows from greed, the sellers' desires to make themselves as well off as possible.

Looking more deeply at figure 2.2, if we fail to produce enough of a good, as at $Q_{\text{Too Little}}$, a little bit more is worth more than it costs to supply. That is, the marginal benefits of more steak exceed the marginal costs of more steak, with an extra pound of steak being worth to steak buyers $18 per pound but only costing steak sellers something less than $6 per pound. Additional steak will continue to make people better off until output is increased to Q^*. At this point the marginal benefits of extra steak equal the marginal costs of extra steak.

In the movement from $Q_{\text{Too Little}}$ to Q^* a net gain in welfare in the steak market is obtained that is equal to area ABC, the net benefits gained from added steak. In the ordinary market case, moreover, at $Q_{\text{Too Little}}$ the high marginal willingness to pay of buyers, relative to the relatively low marginal cost of sellers, will encourage greater steak production—both buyers and sellers are made better off if more steak is produced, so that will happen. Sellers can sell additional steak for more than their costs of production and will want to do so. Greed, in a competitive economy, ends up causing the right amount of goods to be produced.

By an analogous line of reasoning, at $Q_{\text{Too Much}}$, the last unit of steak costs suppliers about $18 per pound, but it is only worth $6 per pound to steak demanders. It is now in the interest of both buyers and sellers if less steak is produced; note, in particular, that sellers must lose money on any steak production in excess of Q^*, because they cannot make buyers pay more for steak than it is worth to them in the voluntary exchange market setting. The welfare loss (cost in excess of benefit) of being at $Q_{\text{Too much}}$ rather than Q^* is seen in figure 2.2 as area CDE.

Q*, then, is seen as the best amount of steak in the sense that either more or less makes those in the steak market worse off. Another way to express this point, to make it clearer to understand, is to consider consumer surplus and producer surplus.

In figure 2.3, we see two approximately triangular areas. One, area P_E BC (with the vertical stripes), is the area above the equilibrium price but below the demand (or marginal willingness to pay) curve. This area shows the net benefit (the consumer surplus) steak buyers get from being able to buy steak at the equilibrium price rather than do without steak entirely, going to zero steak consumption. That is, the last pound of steak consumed in the period is worth to buyers about what they pay for it (that is why it is the last pound consumed). But all of the infra-marginal units are worth more than that, in some cases *much* more than that.[10] The buyer pays the price times quantity for all units consumed, area $OP_E CQ_E$ but retains net benefits of the vertically striped area. In a sense, the main point should be obvious—if consumers are voluntarily buying something it *must* make them better off. They stop buying when they are no longer made better off by an additional purchase, at Q* in figure 2.2.

Similarly, it is only the last unit that a seller supplies that costs as much to supply as the seller receives for it. If they could produce and sell another unit for less than the price they receive, they would do so, because they would have greater profit. To produce and sell a unit that costs more than the price they receive for it would make them worse off, with lower profits. Sellers would have been willing, were it necessary, to sell infra-marginal

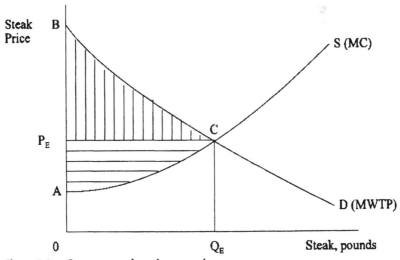

Figure 2.3.   Consumer and producer surplus

units for less but are instead able to sell all units for the going equilibrium price (what the buyers pay is what the sellers receive). As a result they gain area AP_EC in short-run profits, the amount of revenue in excess of their costs.[11] If forced to produce zero output, this area (the producer surplus) is what is lost to the firms.

It is now easy to see why Q_E in figure 2.3 (or Q^* in figure 2.2) is the output level that makes consumers and producers as well off as possible (for ordinary goods with perfect markets). Any other output level, whether larger or smaller, will have a smaller combined area of consumer and producer surplus. There will be a small net benefit (benefit in excess of costs) at any other output level. In the words of Adam Smith in 1776, the market outcome results in the maximum wealth of nations.

Further clarifying, suppose that a law were passed (and enforced) that made it illegal to sell steak for less than $18 per pound, perhaps because of special interest influence of steak suppliers. At that price, resulting in sales of $Q_{Too\ Little}$ in figure 2.2, the net surplus is smaller, although producers might well be better off, because they receive $8 more per pound for the (smaller) quantity demanded versus receiving the equilibrium price of $10 on the (larger) quantity. But consumers are worse off by exactly that same amount—the producer gain is merely a transfer from consumers. And *both* producers and consumers are worse off because goods whose production has positive net benefits to both, in a competitive world, are not produced. The marginal cost of a pound of steak at $Q_{Too\ Little}$ is far below the $18 per pound price, so competitive producers would like to produce more. Consumers would be willing to pay, on the margin, $18 per pound for additional steak, yet it is not forthcoming. Combined producer and consumer surplus is smaller by area ABC in figure 2.2, meaning that the passage of the law has made society *collectively* worse off. The wealth of the nation imposing this price control is lower, though the distribution of the smaller wealth favors the producer in the case depicted.[12]

On the other hand, if consumers had political power, it is possible that price controls might be introduced that capped steak price at about $4.50 per pound (a price that would also result in $Q_{Too\ Little}$ being produced voluntarily, seen at point B of figure 2.2). This might well make consumers better off if they gain in lower prices for the smaller quantity supplied more than they lose by being unable to buy more. But this gain comes at the expense of making producers worse off. The lower price ($4.50 versus $10) helps consumers (or at least those who continue to be able to get the steak they want[13]) but harms firms by exactly the same amount. The same area of overall welfare loss exists at $Q_{Too\ Little}$, area ABC, so society is collectively worse off, but the brunt of the loss is now borne by producers whose surpluses are transferred to consumers.[14]

To further understand the desirable feature of the market outcome for ordinary private goods, return to production possibilities curve discussed in chapter 1. Suppose the two ordinary goods under consideration are steak and t-shirts, as seen in figure 2.4. A society *could* produce any combination of steak and t-shirts along the production possibility curve. At point A relatively large quantities of t-shirts are produced, T_A, which (because of scarcity) means that only a relatively small amount of steak, S_A, can be produced. At point C relatively small quantities of t-shirts are produced, T_C, enabling much larger production of steak, S_C, to be produced. Point B represents an intermediate situation.

Voluntary interactions in competitive markets of uncoerced demanders and suppliers will result in some combination of t-shirts and steak on the production possibility curve, say point B. To emphasize again why B is best, consider any other point, such as A, on the production possibilities frontier of figure 2.4. Suppose that the t-shirt and steak combination represented at point A were imposed on society by a (perhaps well-meaning) government.

The situation is represented in the supply and demand diagrams of figure 2.5. Given true preferences and costs, the welfare loss from too many t-shirts (t-shirts with costs to society, in terms of forgone steak, that are greater than benefits) is shown as the shaded region in the left diagram. The welfare loss from too little steak (steak with benefits to society, in terms of forgone t-shirts, that are greater than costs) is shown as the shaded region in the right diagram. The government, regardless of how well-meaning, is making society worse off—given the preferences of members of society and the costs of producing the various goods. Given the available resources,

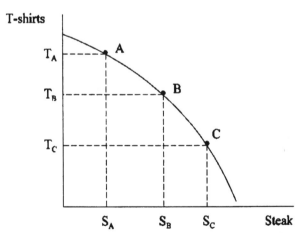

Figure 2.4.   Production possibilities curve for ordinary goods

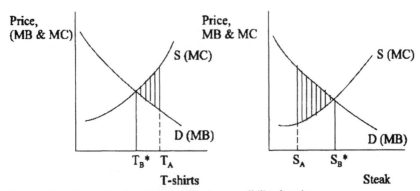

Figure 2.5.   Nonoptimal point on production possibility frontier

only the market-determined relative quantities of t-shirts and steaks, T_B^* and S_B^*, make society as well off as possible. Of the infinite number of possible combinations of t-shirts and steak (the argument applies to all goods, the two-dimensional case just being easy to visualize), the market produces the best one—the one we most want.

The preceding discussion of how perfect markets work to give a society the best relative amounts of all private goods was first convincingly presented by Smith in 1776. He found it remarkable, as many do today, that market prices move in such a way as to act as an "invisible hand," guiding *completely self-interested* buyers (who want lower prices) and *completely self-interested* sellers (who want higher prices) to produce and consume the optimal relative amounts of all ordinary goods. Prices perform three truly remarkable, and vitally necessary (regardless of the economic system being considered), functions simultaneously: First, they *ration* goods to those who value them most highly; second, they *provide information* on the relative scarcity of various goods that is useful to both buyers and sellers; and, third, they provide *incentives* to act on that information, because failing to respond to changed prices means people are not making themselves as well off as possible.

The importance of the role of prices is most easily seen, not in looking at a stable equilibrium price and quantity as we have so far discussed, but when some nonprice variable affects either supply or demand. Imagine an initial price in the steak market that has existed for so long that everyone has adjusted to it. In particular, steak suppliers are just making the normal rate of return on capital invested in steak production—firms will have either entered (if above normal profits were present) or exited (if losses were incurred). Suppose now that income rises, and at this higher income, people want to consume more steak. Figure 2.6 depicts this case. Because of the higher income level, the demand curve shifts rightward, from D_0 to D_1—

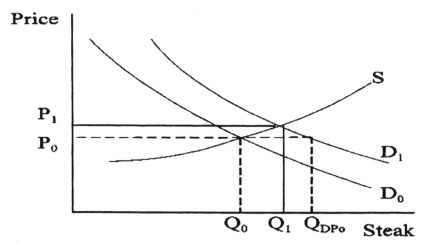

Figure 2.6.   An increase in demand

more steak is demanded at any price, including the original equilibrium price.

The increase in demand causes shortages at the original price P_0, because at that price a much larger quantity, Q_{DP_0}, will be demanded than the quantity that is currently supplied, S_0. As with the previous discussion of forces moving the price to equilibrium, the frustrated buyers—those unable to get steak—will offer more. This will cause the price to begin rising, and two things will happen as a result. First, the higher price will encourage an increased quantity supplied along the unchanged supply curve. Second, the rising price of steak will discourage consumption of steak along the *new* demand curve.

At the new short-run equilibrium, with price, P_1, and quantity, Q_1, consumers will not be getting exactly what they wanted—what they wanted, because of greater income, was a lot more steak at the same price. What they got was some additional steak along with a higher steak price, which they did not want.

But the process that has been set in motion by the increase in income is not yet complete. In the short-run, the rising steak price will serve the function of rationing the steak to those most valuing steak. It will, however, do more than that, because now short-run profitability of steak production has increased. The higher steak prices result in above normal profits that will encourage entry into the steak production industry. Firms will enter until steak production is no more profitable than the production of alternative goods. This will cause the supply curve to shift out in figure 2.6, eventually to where it intersects the new demand curve at the old price.[15] Hence in the long run, the consumer is king, getting what they wanted all along, more steak at the original least-cost price for steak.

For this desirable market result to occur, however, in either the short run or the long run buyers must receive all, and not merely a portion, of the benefits from the goods they buy (or they will buy too little from society's perspective). And more important from the perspective of the environmentalist, sellers must pay all, and not merely a portion, of the costs of the goods they sell (or they will sell too much from society's perspective). That is, if steel sellers pay only for labor, capital, materials, and energy—and not for damages from air pollution, which accompany steel production—apparent marginal costs of steel production will be lower than true costs of steel production and steel will be overproduced. We shall return to this, and other cases of missing markets in great detail in successive chapters.

Like the magician who must somehow sneak the rabbit into the hat before triumphantly pulling it out, the market rabbit only pops out of the hat when all of the assumptions that got him in there are valid. Reiterating, for the market to work to supply consumers with the right amounts of the ordinary goods we want, we must have *many well-informed buyers and sellers each facing the true costs and benefits of their actions*, and not just a portion of the costs and benefits. This might be fairly reasonable for ordinary markets with many repeat purchasers and sellers, but it is more dubious in other contexts as we shall see.

What about equity? Are market outcomes fair? While fairness, like beauty, is in the eyes of the beholder, many people feel that market outcomes are not fair. Some people just function better in market settings than others, being naturally able to produce more of the things people care about (giving them a large income). Others, not necessarily possessing natural advantages in the market system, thrive on its competitiveness and work hard, striving for success (giving them a larger income). Still others, those unfortunate due to circumstances or attitudes, do not thrive in the market system.

There are, however, at least two important considerations. First, some people are going to thrive, while others do not, under *any* system—the advantages given to ranking members of the communist party in the old Soviet Union (special stores to shop in and restricted lanes to drive in, and such) were clearly unfair. In the newly democratized countries of the former Soviet Union, many of the former communist leaders are winning elections, starting businesses, and otherwise thriving in the capitalist system. If fairness is to be judged by outcomes, no system yet devised, or likely to be devised, will have broad-based appeal.

But is it *outcomes* that should be judged as fair or unfair, or is it the rules of the game that should be so judged? Consider a horse race (or a rat race, for that matter). Each horse has an equal opportunity, in the sense that they are carrying the same combined rider and saddle weight.[16] One horse is going to win the race. Suppose the same horse wins the race many times. Should that horse, as a matter of equity, have to carry more weight than the other horses? Most people would say no, because the process is deemed fair—each horse has an equal chance.

Of course, it is not the case that each person has an equal opportunity in the United States or even in the most egalitarian countries of Europe. Inheritance, school quality, natural ability, and many other advantages give some people an edge in any system. As a consequence, the elected officials of most democratic nations intervene, attempting to represent voters' desires for greater fairness. Policies to enhance fairness are instituted, such as various affirmative action programs, welfare, or tax systems, which are by varying amounts progressive (taxing the rich at higher rates than the poor).

Such programs will affect final outcomes, both in terms of the size of the economic pie and how it gets allocated. If people begin to be seen as taking advantage of the dole, public support can, and does, shift to those advocating less egalitarian policies. If the rich seem over time to be prospering relatively more than the poor, public support shifts to more egalitarian policies. If the political party in power ignores such shifting perceptions, it is likely to be replaced in future elections.

But the critical thing to recognize is that all of the desirable features of the market system do not depend on what income distribution is collectively selected. It is true that if a highly progressive income tax is instituted, the market outcomes will *change*—but they will retain the property that they result in the best amounts of the various goods, all other things being equal. For example, with a highly progressive income tax system, the demand for yachts will be much lower—and the market outcome will be that a smaller equilibrium amount of yachts are produced and sold. But, given the politically determined so-called initial endowment, the new, smaller quantity of yachts is the optimal amount.

This follows from the *voluntary* nature of trade stressed in this chapter; whatever income distribution emerges from the political process, market trades will only occur if the parties to them are made better off by trade. As long as the benefits of trade, on the margin, exceed the costs of trade (up to the equilibrium discussed extensively in this chapter), trades will occur making all parties to them wealthier. Indeed, the *prospect* of trade—knowing that it will be possible to trade things one is good at producing for things one is bad at producing—encourages productive specialization, further adding to the wealth-enhancing effects of the market system.

How does the material of this chapter relate to environmental quality? Economists argue that the exact counterpart to a perfectly functioning market outcome for environmental goods comes where marginal social benefits equal marginal social costs. Figure 2.7, depicting this, should look familiar, because it is essentially a supply-and-demand diagram. There is, however, one extremely important difference, one that we shall return to

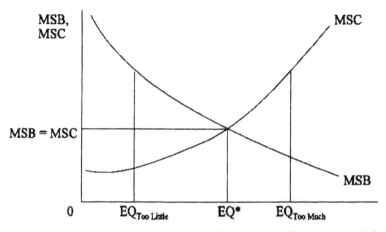

Public Good (Environmental Quality)

Figure 2.7.   Optimal provision for public goods

over and over throughout the book. That difference relates to the nature of public goods, like environmental quality.[17]

Pure public goods have two important properties that differ dramatically from the private goods we have been discussing so far. A pure public good has the twin properties of being *nonrivalrous* and *nonexcludable*. If one person consumes a private good (e.g., steak), another person cannot also consume it. Because of that, the appropriate question regarding how much steak society collectively demands is, "How much steak would society want to buy at various prices?" But in the case of public goods, if one unit of the good is supplied we *all* get to consume it. If our air is cleaner, we all breathe it (and we cannot be excluded from doing so); if the lighthouse exists, we all get to see the light (and we cannot be excluded from doing so); if a species, say the blue whale, is saved, we all get the benefits (and we cannot be excluded from receiving them).

So for pure public goods, the nature of the appropriate question about how much society collectively demands changes to "How much will society value various quantities of the public good (e.g., air quality)?" Looking at figure 2.7, at very low levels of environmental quality, with perhaps many people heavily damaged by pollution and nearly everyone harmed somewhat, the marginal social benefits of increased environmental quality would be high. Each individual benefits in varying amounts, with the rich and sick benefiting greatly from added environmental quality, while even the poor and healthy benefit some. Adding up the benefits each person affected by a policy receives as a result of that policy provides the value to society of a marginal improvement in environmental quality.

Moreover, at such low initial environmental quality levels, because no or few resources are being devoted to the public good, the cost of improving environmental quality (in terms of forgone ordinary goods) is quite low. As we begin cleaning up the environment, the added benefits of still greater cleanup begin falling—the physical damages are less life-threatening and any physical symptoms are felt by an ever-smaller fraction of the population. Additionally, because we must (due to scarcity) transfer resources from the production of private goods to acquire more environmental quality, the reduced amounts of private goods result in their marginal values rising. Hence the costs of extra cleanup become larger the greater the environmental improvement contemplated. As shown in figure 2.7, there will come a point—analogous to the equilibrium for ordinary goods—where the marginal social benefits of further environmental improvement equals the marginal social costs of further environmental improvement. To clean up the environment more than that amount, EQ* in figure 2.7, will make us collectively worse off.[18]

It is now easy to see, as a conceptual matter, why economists want to try to add up the marginal values of environmental quality and compare those to the marginal provision costs. Doing so would provide amounts of public goods that *would* be provided if a perfectly functioning market for environmental goods could exist. Thus, in principle, comparing marginal benefits to marginal costs, going to where MSB = MSC in figure 2.7, would result in the best combination of *both* private and public goods.

For the preceding to hold, as with our assumptions in the discussion of private goods, we must have good information on peoples' preferences for environmental goods relative to other goods, and we must know the available technologies to clean up the environment. That is, we continue to presume that we know the location of the MSB and MSC curves in figure 2.7, because if we do not know the height or slope of either curve, we cannot know how to proceed or how much to clean up the environment. Beginning in chapter 4, the first of these assumptions—that we have a good sense of the value people place on the environment—will be shown to be wildly at odds with reality.

Before turning to the criticisms of the economists' approach that will provide the bulk of the book, we must look at the role of time in economics and the rationale for discounting. In this chapter, the time dimension (that we have largely ignored) was implicitly fairly short-run. The discussion has been about deciding *at a point in time* how many ordinary goods to provide relative to environmental goods. We concluded, for both types of goods, that we would like to go to where the marginal benefits and the marginal costs were equated.

But many decisions involve marginal benefits and marginal costs that occur over many time periods—yet we have to decide what to do now. For example, do we build a dam that will provide irrigation water, electricity, and flood protection? Do we require an expensive smokestack cleaning technology of manufacturers or costly regulations making automobiles cleaner? In such cases, we have to incur costs, possibly large costs, prior to receiving any benefits, and the benefits might continue to take place for many decades. Maintaining the fiction for the time being that we know what the benefits and costs are *in each period*, we turn in chapter 3 to see how those benefits and costs are made comparable—so we can decide what to do *now*—for projects with different time patterns of benefits and costs.

QUESTIONS FOR DISCUSSION

1. What percent of the goods that you desire are wanted because of use values versus nonuse values?
2. Do you think you have more information with which to make informed decisions for ordinary goods or for environmental goods? Why?
3. The steak example (and the later t-shirt example) of the desirability of the market outcome could be flawed, in the sense that the wrong equilibrium amount could exist, if either the demand curve for steak was wrong or the supply curve for steak was wrong. What does *wrong* here mean? Which curve is most likely to be wrong?
4. Marginal willingness to pay can be high either because of great variation in individual preferences (e.g., some people like broccoli a lot while others dislike broccoli but like asparagus a lot) or great variation in individual incomes. Which do you think is most important, tastes or income, in determining MWTP for various goods? Does how important the good is in the budget affect your answer to this question?
5. This chapter discussed voluntary exchanges, but are they truly voluntary? If you are poor but unskilled, you must work—possibly very hard—to acquire a minimal standard of living. Is that work voluntary, in the same way that we often think about volunteering to help a good cause?
6. In the discussion of consumer surplus, would you expect consumer surplus to be larger or smaller if there are good substitutes for the good being considered? Why?
7. Many people advocate interference in market outcomes (e.g., minimum wage, agricultural price supports, rent controls, education subsidies, and so on). Is the desire to interfere driven by concerns of *efficiency* or *equity*? If it came to be widely believed that all people have an equal opportunity to achieve financial success, would such interference become greater or smaller?

8. In this chapter, the market was argued to give people the best quantities of the things they want, given tastes and technology. But are some tastes better than others? If we have tastes for professional wrestling or NASCAR instead of classical music or books on philosophy, more of the former will be produced. Moreover, the market will reward people who produce wrestling or NASCAR, giving them higher incomes, hence the consumption of a larger share of the economic pie. Is this "right?" If one thinks tastes can be questioned, how do we decide what good tastes are versus what bad tastes are? Is there a danger of elitism? (This issue is important to many environmentalists, and particularly matters for public goods, because we are forced to consume the amount that is collectively determined—with NASCAR or classical music, we can each decide. But, for environmental goods, we cannot individually choose.)

9. Looking at figure 2.6, did consumer surplus get larger or smaller at the new equilibrium compared to the old? Did producer surplus get larger or smaller at the new equilibrium compared to the old? Will the change in producer surplus result in firm entry or firm exit in the long run?

10. Suppose, unlike the increase in demand shown in figure 2.6, that there were a decrease in supply. Would consumer surplus rise or fall? Would producer surplus rise or fall? Why?

11. Under what conditions do you feel that you have been treated fairly? What conditions lead you to feel that you have been treated unfairly? Can any generalizations be made from these answers?

NOTES

1. Monetary economics is an exception, with motives for holding money broken into *medium of exchange, asset,* and *precautionary.* Yet even here, these distinctions do not alter what economists do—they look at relative price effects (interest rate differentials in this case) and income effects.

2. Economic historians sometimes provide exceptions. For example, in wondering why we drink relatively large amounts of coffee in the United States, while England drinks relatively large amounts of tea, the historian might attempt to look at consumption levels before and after the Boston Tea Party (the colonists' protest against taxation without representation).

3. Actually the text condition is stronger than necessary, because we are mostly interested in market rather than individual behavior. As long as those who suddenly like something more are roughly offset by those who suddenly like it less, such taste changes will wash out, leaving only relative opportunities to systematically affect behavior. But the key insight is that if tastes are stable, it is only changing opportunities—income and relative prices—that lead to changed behavior.

4. One can easily imagine coming out of a recession, with rising income causing greater demand for cars; the greater demand for cars causing their price to rise,
encouraging a casual observer to conclude that people buy more cars at higher
prices. A rise in income would cause both greater car sales and the higher car prices;
in other cases, some other variable might be confounding the relationship between
price and quantity demanded.

5. The text discussion refers to flow demands and supplies, which inherently
have a per-unit of time dimension, national income and output (gross domestic
product [GDP]) being examples. There are also stock demands and supplies (e.g.,
asset holdings of various types, both private and public) that do not have a time dimension. The sometimes complicated interactions between these concepts are
largely irrelevant to the concerns of this book.

6. This assumption merely ensures that any price increase brought about by
greater demand for some good results in movement of resources into the production of that now more profitable good.

7. An economics joke about price controls has a consumer indignantly com-
plaining to a purveyor of meats, "This is ridiculous! Steak is only $4 per pound just
down the street—how can you have the nerve to charge $12!" To this, the meat mer-
chant replies, "Why don't you buy it down there?" The consumer responds, "Because they are out of meat." "Well," says the meat merchant, "when I'm out of meat,
I'll sell it for $4 per pound, too!"

8. It should probably be pointed out at this juncture that economists have a
long history of putting the price and quantity variables on the wrong axes. The *dependent variable*, quantity demanded or supplied in this case, should by mathemati-
cal convention be put on the vertical y-axis, while the *independent* (or causative) *variable*, price in this case, is conventionally put on the horizontal x-axis. Economists got
that backward eons ago, but like countries considering converting from English
units to Continental metric measurements, the costs associated with switching over
are large. Confusions will turn out to be minor in the present setting.

9. Marginal revenue is not always the same thing as price, but the distinction is
not critical to the discussion here. If an imperfectly competitive firm has to lower
price to sell more, marginal revenue will be below the price charged for the extra
output.

10. Steak almost certainly possesses a "choke-price," a price—perhaps $300 per
pound or so—above which no steak would be sold, with everyone substituting
lower priced sources of protein. In the case of total fluid consumption or total food
consumption there would be no choke-price, and marginal values would explode as
quantities become smaller. If dying of thirst in the desert, Microsoft's Bill Gates
would, if necessary, give millions (perhaps billions) of dollars for a quart of water,
if that quantity of water could get him safely to town versus dying of thirst. It is, of
course, unlikely that he would be charged so much, if he were charged at all—hence
he would gain *immense* consumer surplus from the transaction!

11. In a competitive world the short-run profit, the producer's surplus, will go to
the owner of the fixed factor (capital, but also land). If the rate of return on capital
is greater than normal, it will be profitable for more firms to enter an industry; if the
return on capital is lower than normal, some firms will exit the industry. These firm
considerations are not critical to understanding for the environmental case but are

useful for understanding the long run in which supply curves are quite flat. In the long run, all market surpluses go to the buyer.

12. Producers could also be worse off by the price control, if there are many good substitutes for steak—in extreme cases, they might sell hardly any steak at all—it is unlikely that they would lobby for an $18 per pound price in this case.

13. Discrimination, as to who gets the price-controlled goods, is likely to become important as persons of the disfavored race, sex, or any other characteristic are unable to acquire the steak.

14. Note, too, that by reducing producers' surplus we have lowered the return to capital invested in the steak industry, so some firms will be going out of business in the long run, which will further reduce availability at the controlled price.

15. The text discussion presumes that the resources used in steak production are sufficiently plentiful that expansion of the steak industry does not increase the prices of those resources. To the extent that input prices rise, there will be some positive slope to the long-run supply curve.

16. Weights are added to the saddles of the horses to offset variations in the weight of the riders, guaranteeing that each has an equal opportunity to win.

17. The classic example of a public good is the light from a lighthouse. If the light exists, we all get to see it, benefiting from knowing where the dangerous rocks are.

18. It should be emphasized that, unlike the case of private goods, there will be strongly clashing values among members of society for public goods. If you *really* like a private good, say steak, you will buy lots of it; if you are a vegetarian you do not buy steak at all. There are no clashes of values for private goods, because each individual can consume his or her desired quantities. This is not the case for public goods; indeed, the disagreement about whether we are providing the optimal quantities will be *greatest* when we are near the socially optimal amount. About half the population (those with above average incomes and below average health) will think the environment should be cleaner, while about half will think the costs of more are too great (those with below average incomes and above average health).

3

Benefit-Cost Analysis when Information Is "Perfect": The Role of Time in Environmental Economic Decisions

Benefit-cost analysis, as clarified in the preceding two chapters *as decisions whose benefits and costs take place in a single time period*, has a long history. At heart, it is merely rational thinking, comparing the advantages of various courses of action with the disadvantages. Any decision, including doing nothing, will have advantages and disadvantages, which will occur whether we choose to think about them or not. In voluntary exchanges, ordinary market interactions among suppliers and demanders were seen to lead to the best amounts of ordinary goods. In this chapter we look at the role of time in decision making, examining how to evaluate decisions in which the costs and benefits are received over many time periods into the future. How can we make projects with widely varying patterns of benefits and costs over many time periods comparable, so that we can decide among them? How do we decide *now*?

Prior to delving into the answer to this question a couple of observations must be made. First, in appraising public sector investments one must bear in mind that all projects are not equally important and hence do not merit the same resources for evaluation. And expensive and detailed benefit-cost analysis may itself have costs greater than benefits for inexpensive projects, regardless of the net benefits of the latter. Second, many projects are easily evaluated, clearly having benefits far greater than or far less than costs; such projects can be rejected or accepted without elaborate analysis.

Moreover, for either discrete or continuous decisions, the various advantages and disadvantages need not be converted to dollars, at least in principle (non-money barter being but one example). The impacts of a decision could be left as a long list of positive or negative effects, as seen in the following letter from Ben Franklin written from London on September 19, 1772:

Dear Sir:

In the affair of so much importance to you, wherein you ask my advice, I cannot, for want of sufficient premises, advise you what to determine, but if you please I will tell you how. When those difficult cases occur, they are difficult chiefly because while we have them under consideration, all the reasons pro and con are not present to the mind at the same time; but sometimes one set present themselves, and at other times another, the first being out of sight. Hence the various purposes or inclinations that alternatively prevail, and the uncertainty that perplexes us. To get over this, my way is to divide half a sheet of paper by a line into two columns; writing over the one Pro, and over the other Con. Then, during three or four days consideration, I put down under the different heads short hints of the different motives, that at different times occur to me, for or against the measure. When I have thus got them all together in one view, I endeavor to estimate their respective weights; and where I find two, one on each side, that seem equal, I strike them both out. If I find a reason pro equal to some two reasons con, I strike out the three. If I judge some two reasons con, equal to some three reasons pro, I strike out the five; and thus proceeding I find at length where the balance lies; and if, after a day or two of further consideration, nothing new that is of importance occurs on either side, I come to a determination accordingly. And, though the weight of reasons cannot be taken with the precision of algebraic quantities, yet when each is thus considered, separately and comparatively, and the whole lies before me, I think I can judge better, and am less liable to make a rash step, and in fact I have found great advantage from this kind of equation, in what may be called moral and prudential algebra.

Wishing sincerely that you may determine for the best, I am ever, my dear friend, yours most affectionately,

B. Franklin[1]

Modern benefit-cost analysis merely uses fancy tools in pursuit of Ben Franklin's intuitive decision-making approach. There are only two senses in which benefit-cost analysis as currently practiced differs from Franklin's method, and only one of those is important.

The first difference is that the pros and cons are put in dollar units, and this is of no significance whatsoever. If a pro reason is viewed as equivalent to a con reason, it does not matter whether they are cancelled out as non-monetized effects or as dollar amounts—they still cancel out. The dollars themselves mean nothing as has been emphasized in previous chapters. The use of dollars is sometimes viewed by environmentalists as being crass, base, or inhumane. However, the trade-offs being faced are real, with dollars just being a particularly convenient way to measure them.[2]

The second difference is more important. While not explicitly addressed in Franklin's quote above, the *discount rate* used to make effects occurring in one period comparable to those occurring in another period, possibly a quite removed period, is often critical to the analysis. It matters, and would have mattered to Ben Franklin, if some of the pros or the cons were to occur next year or in one hundred years. Why do economists, and most other people, believe that it is appropriate to weigh benefits and costs that occur in the distant future less, often far less, than benefits that occur more immediately?

To answer this question, we first need to understand what it means when people talk about the interest rate.[3] The interest rate is the price of consuming in this period rather than a year later—it is the forgone benefits of greater future consumption resulting from the decision to consume now. That is, if you consume $1 worth of something in year 0, you will have $(1 + i)$ less of something to consume in year 1, where i is the real rate of interest (subtract the rate of inflation from the nominal interest rate and you have the so-called real interest rate). Conversely, if you save $1 in year 0, you will be able to consume $(1 + i)$ more next year.

Illustrating, if the inflation-adjusted interest rate is 3%, consuming $100 now means that you must forgo $103 worth of real goods next year; saving $100 now allows you to consume $103 more next year. It bears repeating that, just as with any price, the interest rate dollars mean nothing themselves—what is being valued is current consumption relative to future consumption. This is exactly analogous to prices at a point in time that provide relative values of things consumed—you are not really giving up dollars but rather real enjoyment of the second-best thing when you select some other thing to buy, whether at a point in time or over time.

Second, we must recognize how interest rates get determined. As with any price, interest rates are determined in a market by voluntary exchanges among demanders and suppliers. In this case, the market is the loanable funds market in which households are the suppliers of loanable funds, and firms are the demanders of loanable funds.[4] Why do households and firms enter this market to borrow and lend money?

Consider first, savers. All saving is done, ultimately, because of desires for future consumption. The saving might be a hedge against the risks of lost income, hence consumption, inherent in an uncertain future (e.g., becoming unemployed or disabled and unable to work). Or the saving might fund a possibly lengthy period of retirement, when consumption must be maintained without earned income. Moreover, because we do not know exactly how long we will live, and we do not want to run out of income, there is likely to be wealth left over when the average person dies. Also, saving might occur to provide for greater future consumption by one's heirs, a so-called bequest motive. So people save for many reasons, and the question arises "How responsive is savings to changes in its price, the interest rate?" It turns out that savings is not responsive to changes in interest rates.

On the one hand, if interest rates go up, it costs us more, in terms of for-gone future consumption, to consume now. This effect should cause people to consume less and save more now, because higher interest rates reward savers with greater future consumption. But suppose you are saving for some specific future wealth goal (e.g., a house down payment, buying a new car, or having a certain amount of amassed wealth for retirement). Higher interest rates mean that a *smaller* amount of saving now will cumulate to any fixed dollar amount in the future. The net effect is that saving is not ter-ribly responsive to interest rates, hence the supply of loanable funds is drawn as only slightly upward sloping in figure 3.1.

Some savers send funds directly to borrowers (purchases of corporate stocks and bonds do this). Other savers put funds into accounts set up by financial intermediaries (banks, savings and loans, mutual funds, and such), and the latter route those funds on to various borrowers. Why do de-manders of loanable funds enter that market wanting to borrow money?

Borrowers are borrowing, because they value the profits that (they hope) can be obtained by using those funds productively (e.g., buying machines or factory/office buildings).[5] Borrowers would generally be expected to de-mand fewer funds at higher interest rates (fewer investment projects will be profitable if the costs of borrowing increase). Thus, the interest rate in a so-ciety, while seemingly just a financial or dollar thing, really represents the interaction between productivity and thrift.

The equilibrium interest rate, i_e, exists when the interest rate moves to equate the supply and the demand for loanable funds, by the usual forces discussed in chapter 2. Very thrifty societies will have lower interest rates (the supply of loanable funds in figure 3.1 will be shifted further to the

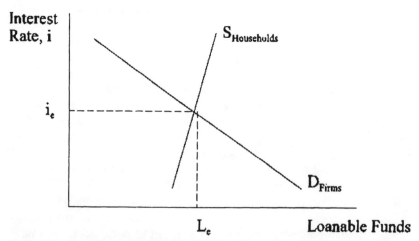

Figure 3.1.   Interest rates resulting from the interaction of productivity and thrift

right), while societies with many productive investments will have higher interest rates (the demand for loanable funds in figure 3.1 will be shifted further to the right).

As with price in any market, buyers (in this case, borrowers) would like to pay less, while sellers (in this case, savers) would like to receive a higher price. As always, the equilibrium price balances these desires, leaving both demanders and suppliers—while not necessarily happy—at least able to do what they want to do at the price they face. If not interfered with, the loanable funds market will clear, and the market-clearing interest rate will have a critical property. That critical property is that the interest rate provides the link between present periods and future periods. This link will be seen to enable us to make efficient decisions (decisions with benefits greater than costs) *now* about projects that have widely varying patterns of benefits and costs in the future.

That the interest rate is positive in figure 3.1 implies that all other things being equal, our preferences are such that we would prefer to have things now rather than later. Another way to express this is that we have to be bribed with greater future consumption to be willing to give up current consumption. We are said to have a positive rate of time preference. It is just in the nature of our preferences, like enjoying pleasant views or high fat ice cream. If we were to suddenly like future goods consumption relatively more vis-à-vis current consumption, we would save more than we do now, leading to a lower interest rate—we would not need to be bribed as much to give up current consumption.

As with ordinary markets at a point in time, efficient decisions are not necessarily equitable decisions. One might argue that it is unfair that caviar, diamonds, and yachts are produced for the rich in a time period in which some poor are going homeless despite the efficiency of the equilibrium quantities in those markets. Similarly, some efficient decisions over long time periods will harm future generations that we care about, while other equally efficient decisions will not.[6] And just as at a point in time we may sacrifice efficiency for greater equity (e.g., not requiring engine replacement or scrapping of cars that fail tailpipe emission inspections, because such cars are predominantly owned by the poor), it is possible that we might prefer a long-term project that is inefficient, because we like its equity impact.

So how do interest rates work to help us decide which projects among many potential projects to pursue now on efficiency grounds? First, one needs to recognize that discounting is just the flip side of compounding. Because interest rates are positive, any amount loaned out today will become worth more in the future. But, if $1 today grows through compounding to $1+ i one year from now, the logical conclusion is that $1 received one year from now must be worth *less* than $1 today (because we know $1 today will, in fact, be worth $1+ i next year).[7]

Illustrating, at 10% interest, $1 next year is only worth about $0.91 now because $0.91 can be put in an interest-earning asset and by earning $0.091 become approximately $1 next year. If you were to pay much more than $0.91 you would be foolish in that you would be getting a below normal return on your investment. If, for example, you were will to pay $0.95 now for $1 next year, you would only be getting about 5% rather than the 10% you could obtain (at 10%, $0.95 could earn $.095 in interest, hence you could have had $1.045 at the end of the year but are getting only $1). If you were to pay much less, that would be great (for you), but the borrower would be paying more in interest than necessary. That is, if you could buy the $1 next year for only $0.83 now that would result in a 20% interest payment (20% of $0.83 is approximately $0.17). A rational borrower would never sell the claim on $1 next year so cheaply, because he or she is paying 20% interest when funds can be had for only 10%.

Further clarifying, a dollar next year is worth less now—is said to have a present value less than a dollar—because some amount less than a dollar now (how much less depends on the rate of interest) will compound into a dollar in the future according to the following formula:

3.1 $$X(1+i) = \$1$$

where X is the present value of the $1 in one year. That is, X shows the amount of money *now* that will grow to $1 next year at various interest rates. Solving for X, we get:

3.2 $$X = \$1/(1+i)$$

In our earlier example, X = $0.91 when i = 0.10 or 10%. The present value, X, is the discounted value of a dollar to be received next year.

What if you receive that $1 not one year from now but two years from now? Well, you only have to figure out what amount will cumulate to $0.91 at the end of the first year, because you already know that $0.91 will become $1 in one more year. So, you realize that $0.83 will do that—after the first year you will have $.83(1+0.10) = $0.83 + $0.083 = $0.91+. By the end of the next year, $0.83 will, then, grow to become $1 according to:

3.3 $$X(1+i)(1+i) = \$1$$

where X is the present value of the $1 to be received in two years. In our example, X = $0.83 when i = 0.10 or 10%. Solving for X, we arrive at:

3.4 $$X = \$1/[(1+i)(1+i)] = \$1/(1+i)^2$$

More generally, $1 received in any period, say period t, is worth today:

3.5 $$X = \$1/(1+i)^t$$

because X will grow to be $1 in t periods. The further into the future a dollar's worth of benefit is received (or a dollar's worth of cost is paid) the less it is worth now, because the denominator in the above expression gets bigger as t gets bigger (because $1 + i$ is greater than 1). Only if interest rates were zero would future benefits and costs not be discounted.

We are now ready to understand how benefit-cost analysis is conducted, because every project investment is merely a stream of dollar benefits or costs that occur over some number of periods. That is, if $C in costs occur in the second year, they have a present value of $C/(1+i)^2$. If there are $B in benefits that occur in the sixth year, they have a present value of $B/(1+i)^6$. To evaluate various projects we need only add up all the present values of all the benefits and costs that occur in each period for the life of the project and see if the resulting number is greater than or less than zero. Remember that the dollars, themselves, mean nothing—it is real goods, things that we care about, that are ultimately being compared. Benefit-cost analysis for long-term projects is exactly analogous, in terms of its efficiency properties, to supply and demand at a point in time.

If the sum of the present values of all benefits and costs is greater than zero, the project is said to have a positive net present value (NPV) and should—on efficiency grounds—be adopted. If on the other hand, the NPV is less than zero, the project will lower the value of our scarce resources, returning less than alternative projects. Social welfare will be lower than it could be and the project is said to be inefficient for that reason. It has costs greater than benefits when both are properly counted and converted into present values. As an illustrative example, to ensure that the preceding is clear, consider the following simple hypothetical project with a typical pattern of benefits and costs, in this case extending only over five years (see table 3.1).

The first observation about the hypothetical project represented by the numbers in table 3.1 is that their pattern is reasonable. Costs have to be incurred (the $5,000 and $2,100 in the first and second period) before any benefits can be experienced (benefits begin in period two and continue for four periods). Also, we typically have maintenance costs throughout the lifetime of a project that are necessary to continue receiving the benefits. This general pattern holds whether we are building a manufacturing plant to produce blue jeans, building a dam for irrigation, flood protection, or

Table 3.1.　Ilustrative Benefit-Cost Project Analysis

Period	0	1	2	3	4	5
B	-0-	-0-	$3,205	$4,472	$3,430	$2,275
C	$5,000	$2,100	$1,000	$1,000	$1,000	$1,000
NB	–$5,000	–$2,100	+$2,205	+$3,472	+$2,430	+$1,276
DF (5%)	1.0	0.952	0.907	0.864	0.823	0.784
NPV	–$5,000	–$2,000	+$2,000	+$3,000	+$2,000	+$1,000

NB, net benefits; DF, discount factor

electricity generation, or putting catalytic converters on cars to obtain cleaner air.

The fifth row in table 3.1 shows the discount factor to be applied to benefits and costs (or more simply to apply to the net benefits in each period). For simplicity, 5% is used as the discount rate, though we shall later see that the actual rate chosen is controversial. Costs occurring in the first period (now) are not discounted, because they are not in the future. The costs that occur in the next period, period one, are discounted by 0.952, because $1/(1 + 0.05) = 0.952$, a specific case of the earlier general formula of equation 3.5. Similarly, a dollar's worth of benefits or costs occurring in period two are worth only $1/(1 + 0.05)^2 = 0.907$ now, and so on, with net benefits that take place in more distant periods being worth progressively less now.

The hypothetical benefit numbers were "rigged" in table 3.1 to result in nice, simple numbers for the discounted net benefits in the bottom row of the table. Because the numbers in the bottom row have all been discounted, we can just add them up to determine the overall NPV of the hypothetical project. That NPV is $1,000, which is greater than zero, hence the project in question is an efficient project and will make society collectively better off.

Using summation notation, the information in table 3.1 can compactly be represented as:

3.6 $\Sigma\ [(B_t - C_t)/(1 + i)^t] = NPV\ (=\$1,000\ in\ our\ example)$

That is, you just sum over all t periods the discounted net benefits in each period. This compact equation neatly captures all of the information in table 3.1. For $t = 0$, $(B_0 - C_0)/(1 + i)^0$ is just $(0 - \$5,000)/1 = -\$5,000$, the first number in the bottom row. For $t = 1$, $(B_1 - C_1)/(1 + i)^1$ becomes $(0 - \$2,100)/(1 + 0.05)^1 = -\$2,000$, and so on. It will be useful to continue with the rest of the time periods to be certain that you understand how equation 3.6 reflects the information in table 3.1.

The intuition for why we are better off accepting projects with positive NPVs comes from the fact that we discounted, at least ideally, the benefits and costs at the opportunity cost of the funds invested. If we can earn 5% on alternative projects, we would not like to earn only 3% or 4% on the project under consideration. But by using 5% as our discount rate, a positive NPV means that we are doing *better*—earning a higher return on our project—than we could earn on alternative assets. Indeed, if our hypothetical project's benefits and costs both ended in period four, the NPV would equal zero, so we would still be indifferent between the project and the alternative asset.

So the first of the three decision-making rules to be understood, for projects with benefits and costs occurring over many time periods, is simple:

Rule #1: Never accept a project unless its NPV > 0 (we are indifferent if NPV = zero).

Sometimes an agency, whether the Environmental Protection Agency or the Department of Defense, has a budget constraint that is unrelated to how many good projects it might wish to pursue. This leads to a second decision-making rule that is only slightly more complicated than Rule #1:

Rule #2: When budget constrained, pick the subset of projects that maximizes NPV.

Illustrating this rule with an example, consider the following four independent[8] projects, where PVC is the present value of the costs of the projects (see table 3.2).

You would like to accept all of these projects (Rule #1), but suppose you only have $4 million to spend. You could proceed with projects A and B, or you could proceed with C and D. You would love to be able to pursue projects B and D (getting $685,000 in net benefits), but those projects would cost $5 million and you only have $4 million to spend. In this illustrative example, you would adopt projects A and B, because you get the highest net benefit for society that you can with your $4 million ($460,000). The alternative affordable projects C and D only yield $375,000 in NPV, hence are inferior to A and B on efficiency grounds.[9]

The final decision-making rule of this chapter is going to be *much* more confusing to understand but is nonetheless important for environmentalists (and others) to know. In many cases, projects are *mutually exclusive* in the sense that if you pursue one project, you cannot do another. You cannot, for example, simultaneously decide to have a four-lane highway and a six-lane highway at the same location. Or you cannot simultaneously have a gravel road, an asphalt road, and a concrete road but rather must pick between them, where they differ greatly in the time pattern of construction costs and maintenance costs. In the environmental context, you might be considering three control technologies for the same environmental problem, where only one of the approaches is to be selected to ameliorate the problem.

In such mutually exclusive cases, the appropriate decision rule will initially seem plausible and to parallel earlier rules but will be seen to have some counterintuitive—yet important—implications. In particular, the rule will reveal that *under certain circumstances* (in the present setting, where

Table 3.2.   Maximize Portfolio when Budget Constrained

	PVC	NPV
Project A	$1 million	+$50,000
Project B	$3 million	+$410,000
Project C	$2 million	+$100,000
Project D	$2 million	+$275,000

projects are mutually exclusive), NPV can rank projects differently from some commonly used alternative decision rules (benefit-cost ratios and internal rate of return). Rule number three:

Rule #3: Among mutually exclusive projects, pick the maximum NPV project.
Illustrating Rule #3, consider the following projects (see table 3.3).

Which project would you want to pursue? Your initial reaction is to reject Project E in favor of Project G because you get twice the net present value ($600,000 versus $300,000) at only 50% more cost. That is fine, because Project G also has a bigger NPV. Project F, on the other hand, is more than twice as expensive as Project G but only gets one-third more in NPV. You might be tempted to pursue Project G, on efficiency grounds, over Project F.

Perhaps startlingly, project F is the most efficient project of the three! Project G is not as good as Project F, though this result is, as already mentioned, quite counterintuitive for most people. If you understand why Project F is best among the three projects (indeed, it would be better even if Project G had an NPV of $799,999), you are well on your way to understanding how to decide what to invest in now, the question this chapter opened with.

There are several ways to get intuition about the superiority of Project F over Project G. First, suppose you chose Project G and merely invested the leftover $2.5 million, earning say 5%. Because a 5% opportunity cost of the funds was used to discount the projects, the $2.5 million used elsewhere would have an NPV of exactly zero. In other words, while we added another $2.5 million to the PVC in going from Project G to Project F, we also added $2.7 million to the present value of benefits—hence the $2.5 million increase in project size or quality returned $200,000 over and above the opportunity cost of the funds.

This is clearer if we think more about what NPV really means. NPV of the project is the same as the difference between the present value of benefits, PVB, and the PVC. Breaking the benefits and costs apart yields:

$$3.7 \quad NPV = \Sigma[(B_t - C_t)/(1 + i)^t] = \Sigma[(B_t)/(1 + i)^t] - \Sigma[(-C_t)/(1 + i)^t]$$
$$= PVB\text{-}PVC$$

In other words, the efficient outcome—recall the consumer and producer surplus discussion of chapter 2—is not to maximize NPV per dollar of cost

Table 3.3.   Maximize NPV for Mutually Exclusive Projects, Regardless of Benefit-Cost Ratios

	PVC	NPV
Project E	$1 million	+$300,000
Project F	$4 million	+$800,000
Project G	$1.5 million	+$600,000

but rather to maximize NPV, period. Consider some unspecified ordinary market good as shown in figure 3.2. Imagining the three quantities on the horizontal axis as being discrete policies to choose among, which one is the best policy, the most efficient policy? Clearly it is policy 3, because that policy makes us as well off as possible given our tastes and technology. Were we to stop well short of that quantity, say at policy 1, we would have more benefits *per dollar spent*, and a high benefit-to-cost ratio, but we would not be making ourselves as well off as possible. Moving from policy 1 to policy 2 would make us better off, because the marginal benefits would exceed the marginal costs by the horizontally cross-hatched area in figure 3.2. Note that the benefit-cost ratio—the ratio of the area under the (falling) demand curve to the area under the (rising) supply curve—would be smaller at policy 2 than at policy 1. Net benefit is maximized with policy 3.

Yet another analogy to aid intuition comes from microeconomic principles of the theory of the firm where the goal is not to maximize profit *per unit* but rather total profit (revenue *minus* cost, not revenue *over* either cost or quantity).[10] General Motors might make the most money *per car* by restricting output to a small level. However, *total* profit would be much smaller at that point, because cars with low marginal cost relative to marginal benefit (marginal revenue, in this case) are not produced.

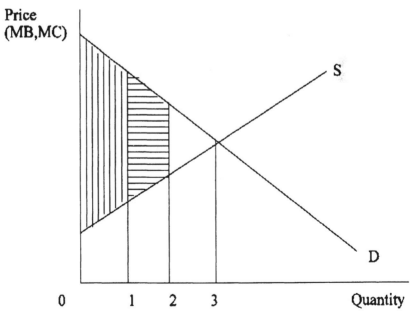

Figure 3.2. Net benefits matter, not ratios of benefits to costs

Return to figure 3.2 and now think in terms of a discrete mutually exclusive public policy decision. For example, policies 1, 2, or 3 could be the decision to have one, two, or three lanes in each direction on a highway. The benefits of having one lane in each direction are large, enabling people to get from location A to location B. But adding an extra lane (policy 2) might well have benefits greater than costs, particularly as population and income grow, increasing the benefit of the time savings associated with the extra lanes. If, as shown, the benefits are sufficiently high relative to the costs of a marginal lane, policy 3, having three lanes in each direction, might be optimal.

Similarly, and more relevantly for the purposes of environmental economics, policies 1, 2, and 3 might represent choices among increasingly stringent air pollution cleanup policies. An inexpensive policy might have substantial benefits in cleaning up the air relative to its costs, but as long as the marginal benefits exceed the marginal costs, additional cleanup is justified on efficiency grounds. These examples make clear that a benefit-cost analysis is not a one-time thing—cleaning up the air will have greater benefits if there are more people to experience them or if those that do have a greater willingness to pay because of income growth. An environmental project that might have looked inefficient (C > B) twenty years ago might have benefits far in excess of costs at this time.

The lesson from Rule #3 is that it is NPV and *not* benefit-cost ratio (or internal rate of return, as we shall see) that should be used to decide among mutually exclusive projects. These other approaches are often presented in court testimony as indicating that a stringent environmental control is inferior to a more lax control. Equation 3.8 defines the benefit-cost ratio:

3.8 $\qquad \Sigma[(B_t)/(1 + i)^t]/ \Sigma[(C_t)/(1 + i)^t] = PVB/PVC$

The benefit-cost decision criterion, often thought to be equivalent to Rule #1 for NPV, is that one should do any project with a benefit-cost ratio greater than or equal to 1. After all, if the ratio of a numerator and a denominator is greater than or equal to unity, the NPV must be greater than or equal to zero, so the two rules might seem to be merely different ways of saying the same thing.

If all projects were continuous and unrelated, benefit-cost ratios would rank projects exactly as NPV would. But as is clear from mutually exclusive Projects E, F, and G, this is not always the case. Project E has a benefit-cost ratio of 1.3 ($1.3 million in PVB and $1 million in PVC, for an NPV of $300,000), and Project G has a benefit-cost ratio of 1.4 ($2.1 million in PVB and $1.5 million in PVC, for an NPV of $600,000). Project F, the preferred project, only has a benefit-cost ratio of 1.2 ($4.8 million in PVB and $4 million in PVC, for an NPV of $800,000), well below either of the other projects—yet it is preferred on efficiency grounds!

Turning to the internal rate of return (IRR) it is defined as follows:

3.9 $\Sigma[(B_t - C_t)/(1 + k)^t] = 0$, where k is solved for as the IRR[11]

Instead of discounting by the opportunity cost of funds and exploring whether the NPV is greater than zero or not, this approach determines a discount rate that just equates the PVB and PVC. The IRR decision criterion, again often thought to be equivalent to Rule #1 for NPV, is that one should do any project with an IRR greater than the opportunity cost of the funds, *i*. After all, any project with a higher rate of return than the opportunity cost of the funds must also, as a logical matter, have a positive NPV.

However, IRR suffers from the same flaw as the benefit-cost ratio in cases of mutually exclusive projects. Projects that are too small or of low quality will often have higher IRR, because a relatively large amount of benefits can be had at low cost in such cases, as shown in figure 3.2. Expanding the size or quality of the project—even when the (falling) marginal benefits of doing so exceed the (rising) marginal costs—will lower the IRR.

In looking at equations 3.7, 3.8, and 3.9 what is striking is that *exactly* the same information is required to make decisions under all three decision criteria. There is, in other words, no reason whatsoever to prefer benefit-cost ratios or IRR to NPV, because there are situations in which the other approaches will not properly rank projects, but NPV always will.[12]

As with chapters 1 and 2, this chapter has made a number of strong, and optimistic, assumptions. First, we have assumed that we actually *know* with certainty the benefits and costs occurring in each period. We did this to focus exclusively on the role of time, avoiding what we will see are important practical considerations. As we shall see in the remainder of the book it is difficult to know what is in the numerators of a benefit-cost analysis and even the choice of discount rate is controversial.

Moreover, as in previous chapters, we assume in this chapter that political considerations will not distort the decision-making process. In the case of ordinary goods, unfettered supply and demand yield outcomes that are efficient, which result in production and consumption of goods up to the point where marginal benefits just equal marginal costs. The government was assumed to want to replicate this efficient process for (public) goods that cannot be profitably supplied privately, producing quantities at which marginal benefits equal marginal costs. Similarly we are assuming here that the government will wish to provide the long-term projects that are optimal for its citizens, at least attempting to accurately gauge benefits and costs in the numerator and to use the appropriate discount rate, given our rate of time preference.

However, in real world benefit-cost analyses, particularly for environmental projects with uncertain benefits and costs, powerful vested interests might want to distort the analysis. If those vested interests want to pursue a project, say a dam, they will advance arguments for high benefits of flood protection, irrigation, and electricity while downplaying costs. If the vested interests do not want to pursue a project, say the addition of catalytic converters to automobiles, they will claim benefits to air quality are lower and costs are higher than either truly are. Benefit-cost analysis can be, and has been, used to justify many bad projects and to discredit many good projects.

Issues of preferences over preferences discussed in chapters 1 and 2 also persist here. Just as environmentalists are likely to have disdain for many goods people demand at a point in time (e.g., sport utility vehicles [SUVs], sprawling mega-mansions, and the like) they are also likely to disapprove of peoples' rates of time preference. Positive discount rates reflect a desire to consume goods *now* with less concern about *future* goods of any kind, environmental or ordinary. Hence, a reasonable fear is that outcomes emerging from benefit-cost analyses might result in unsustainable futures with ecosystem collapse and perhaps the demise of the human species. Also, the numerators in benefit-cost analyses of long-term projects reflect the same preferences that concern environmentalists at a point in time. Environmentalists might see benefit-cost analysis as a fancy technique to rubber-stamp faulty preferences and preconceived biases. In the words of Stanislaw J. Lec, "Is it progress if a cannibal uses a knife and fork?"[13] Still, who among us thinks our preferences are wrong and in need of change? If we really felt that way, we could always change our preferences.

To summarize this chapter, properly conducted benefit-cost analysis has the same desirable features, for projects with an important time dimension, as ordinary supply and demand does at a point in time. If we possess perfect information about preferences, available technology, and all prices (including the appropriate discount rate), we should make perfect decisions. Decisions would be perfect cross-sectionally, with both private and public goods being produced at levels that equate marginal benefits with marginal costs at a point in time. But decisions would also be perfect intertemporally, with benefit-cost analyses optimally allocating our capital among long-term projects, by entrepreneurs for private goods and by government for public goods.

QUESTIONS FOR DISCUSSION

1. Many countries currently have, or have had at some point, usury laws to protect borrowers from exorbitant interest rate charges by lenders. In the context of figure 3.1, what impact would you expect such laws to have on the amount of loanable funds exchanged? Would this be good or bad for a country's growth prospects?

2. How do you feel about intergenerational equity? Will individuals of the future be richer or poorer than individuals of the present? Is just wealth at stake or do irreversible decisions (e.g., the loss of a species) impact how you feel about intergenerational equity?
3. If the true discount rate is suddenly realized to be substantially smaller or larger than had been thought, how would this affect the rankings of various projects? Would an environmental project with distant benefits and high current costs (e.g., global warming) be more or less favored?
4. In this chapter we have assumed that the numerators are known with certainty, to focus on the pure role of time. How badly conducted do you think benefit-cost analyses would have to be before you would feel that this technique should not be used at all? But, if we do not use benefit-cost analysis, how can we decide among the many long-term projects that environmentalists and others advance?

NOTES

1. Benjamin Franklin, "Letter to Joseph Priestley," in *Benjamin Franklin: Representative Selections, with Introduction, Bibliography, and Notes*, eds., Frank Luther Mott and Chester E. Jorgenson (New York: American Book Company, 1936), 348–49.
2. Many of the costs (e.g., for a catalytic converter on a car or a scrubber for a smokestack) automatically come in the form of dollars. Similarly, labor maintenance costs of such equipment are also most conveniently measured in dollars. These costs (disadvantages) must be compared to the benefits (advantages) regardless of the units of measurement.
3. There are, of course, a great many different interest rates (federal funds rate, prime rate, mortgage rate, Treasury bill rate, and so on) which vary in magnitude according to risk, length of borrowing period, and so on. But greed will cause them to all move up or down together (if an asset promised an unusually high interest return, investors would attempt to buy it in preference to other assets, which would drive up its price, lowering the yield to that of other assets).
4. There are two minor complications. First, some households are not suppliers of loanable funds but rather are demanders of loanable funds supplied by other households. This occurs for a variety of reasons (stage in life cycle, unusual circumstances, such as loss of a job, and so on). To take care of this, we will just net out the household borrowers, so that we can better isolate the determinants of the interest rate. The second complication is that the Federal Reserve can, at least temporarily, enter the loanable funds market as either a supplier of loanable funds (when it buys bonds from the private sector by making so-called open market purchases) or as a demander of loanable funds (when it sells bonds to the private sector, an open market sale). These actions are employed in an attempt to stabilize the short-run fluctuations of the economy, but they have little long-term impact, because permanent increases in money result in increased inflation while permanent decreases result in

decreased inflation. The Federal Reserve has no *real* impact in the long run, because money cannot make things, though people can with resources.

5. Governments also enter the loanable funds market as either suppliers (rarely these days) or demanders (often, particularly at the federal level in recent years). While more complicated to explain in detail than can be justified for current purposes, taxes must ultimately be raised to pay back government borrowing and interest on borrowing. If rational, households would be expected, as a first approximation, to save in anticipation of their greater future tax liability. Thus, government borrowing should result in increased saving of roughly equal magnitude, leaving only business borrowers as the driving force on the demand side of the loanable funds market. Among macroeconomists the preceding assertion (the importance of what is called Ricardian equivalence) is hotly debated, and crowding out is clearly a possibility (greater government demand raising interest rates, leading to reduced demands from private firms). None of this is terribly important for purposes of environmental economics, although anything that affects real interest rates will be seen to have an impact on benefit-cost analysis.

6. It is, of course, not the least bit clear that we should care more or less than we do about any particular generation. It is quite possible that future generations will be much better off than we are currently, in which case a specific equity concern for their welfare might involve transfers from the poor (households now) to the rich (households in the future). As always, equity is in the eyes of the beholder, though we shall return to this point in greater detail later in the book.

7. While the text discussion is about $1, the discussion applies to any dollar amount (e.g., $W will grow to $W[1 + i] in one year).

8. It is possible that adopting one of the projects could lower or raise the NPVs of other projects, an unnecessary complication for present purposes.

9. As always, projects C and D might be preferred on equity grounds, because equity is in the eyes of the beholder, an ethical issue about which little can be said formally.

10. Maximum profit per unit always occurs at lower output levels than maximum total profit except in the long-run equilibrium where the proper rule for maximizing profit (produce until marginal cost equals price) happens to coincide with the erroneous one (because marginal cost happens to equal average total cost at the latter curve's minimum).

11. In general, of course, there will be many solutions to this equation (a tth degree polynomial), which further adds unnecessary interpretive complications.

12. Another decision-making mechanism, the payback period, is also sometimes discussed. Under this approach, whichever project returns its investment most quickly is preferred. This approach is demonstrably inferior to any of the mechanisms for evaluating projects discussed in the text, in many cases even violating Rule #1.

13. Stanislaw J. Lec, *Unkempt Thoughts* (New York: St. Martin's Press, 1972), 160.

II

"MISSING MARKETS": EXTERNALITIES, PUBLIC GOODS, AND PROPERTY RIGHTS

The previous three chapters have described how a perfectly functioning market system works and why it results in quantities of ordinary goods that make human beings as well off as possible, both at a point in time and over time. This desirable outcome assumes that human tastes, production technology, and equilibrium prices are known.

Moreover, it was seen in these chapters that producing public goods at levels where (aggregate) marginal social benefits equal marginal social provision costs yields an outcome that shares the desirable efficiency properties of perfect markets for private goods. It would seem that all we have to do is add up individual marginal benefits and merely compare them to marginal costs and do all activities with marginal benefits greater than marginal costs. To decide what long-term investments—public or private—to pursue, it would seem that the same decision-making rules that apply to private goods also apply to public goods, namely, invest if NPV is greater than zero.

There are many reasons, however, to suspect that performing these calculations will be far more difficult for public goods than for private goods. For private goods you must reveal your true marginal willingness-to-pay (paying the market price); otherwise you are unable to obtain the good. Similarly, a seller has an incentive to supply any good that has a marginal cost lower than the marginal revenue obtained by a sale.

In Part II, we discuss the role of "missing markets," situations where markets do not exist or where the equilibrium marginal price is not related to either marginal social benefits or marginal social costs. In such cases, incentives become distorted, and buyers and sellers exchange quantities that end up making us collectively worse off. I prefer to call the problems discussed in this part missing markets, rather than the more traditional "market failures," because the problems really represent a *failure to have markets* and not a failure associated with markets per se. It is just that certain markets are unable to exist.

Chapter 4 considers the implications of situations where either buyers or sellers do not receive all the marginal benefits or pay all the marginal costs of their actions. We shall see, not surprisingly, that if buyers do not receive all of the benefits from buying a good they will buy an amount that society deems nonoptimal. A simple environmental example would be the purchase of ladybugs to eliminate aphids from rosebushes. Many ladybugs will go to other households' backyards and eat their aphids, yielding benefits to society that might not be considered by the purchasers, particularly if they are not fond of their neighbors. Goods giving rise to *positive externalities*, such as this ladybug case (or more important cases such as years of education), will be underpurchased and underconsumed from society's perspective relative to the greater optimal purchase quantities.

Similarly, if consumers damage other households (e.g., noise damage from loud music or pollution from a fireplace) they will tend to overpurchase and overconsume. This follows from the fact that their private benefits overstate full social benefits, because their actions lower benefits others receive by the so-called *negative externalities*.

Usually, when people think about environmental problems, however, they are thinking about firm behavior. When sellers do not pay all of the marginal costs associated with producing their good (e.g., a steel producer not considering its air pollution damage), they will tend to overproduce goods relative to the socially optimal amount of production. The true marginal costs will exceed the marginal costs paid by the seller, so a profit-maximizing seller will end up selling goods that have marginal social costs greater than marginal social benefits. Chapter 4 discusses in detail the problems caused by externalities of every kind and the natural policy response to dealing with these problems. That policy response is to "internalize the externality" (introduce taxes or subsidies that result in buyers and sellers seeing the true costs of their actions, eliminating the missing market), or to directly regulate behavior. But, as will be clear in later chapters it is difficult to know how big externalities actually are in real-world cases.

In chapter 5, we return to discussion of public goods, recognizing that such goods result in another sort of missing market problem. Here the problem is the inability to sell a product to someone if they cannot be prevented from consuming that product without paying. Illustrating, if you were to install a large and costly filter to clean up the air in a community, you cannot earn any revenue from your efforts, because others can consume the clean air whether they pay you or not. In fact, it would be irrational for people to pay in such situations (though perhaps some public-spirited individuals might pay), hence you would abandon your project. The air would go uncleaned, even in cases in which the true marginal benefits were vastly in excess of the true marginal costs, because the supplier cannot force households to pay for the benefits they receive.

Externalities and public goods are related because externalities tend to occur in public good media (e.g., air or noise pollution, CO_2 buildup). One is much more likely to find graffiti in a public restroom than in the bathroom of a private home, because private owners have an incentive to take care of the assets that they own.

The Coase Theorem,[1] as a potential means of solving problems of externalities and public goods provision, is discussed in chapter 6. In this chapter it is seen that *under certain circumstances* voluntary transactions between those damaged and those doing the damage would be expected to automatically solve missing market problems. The circumstances under which the Coase Theorem is operable, however, are somewhat limited. Ronald Coase's argument may best be thought of as providing a reason why there are not more environmental problems than there are. For example, your neighbors might burn firewood in their fireplaces, damaging you, but they are much less likely to dump trash over the fence separating your properties. This is because property rights are clear in the case of land (deeds of ownership exist) and compensatory and punitive damages can be awarded at low cost by courts to the damaged party. It is much more difficult to know whose air is whose or how much damage is due to any one polluter.

NOTE

1. Ronald Coase, "The Problem of Social Cost," *Journal of Law and Economics* 3 (October 1960): 1–44.

4

Externalities as Missing Markets

Recall from previous chapters that suppliers will supply goods as long as their marginal cost is less than or equal to the price they receive and that demanders will demand goods as long as their marginal benefit is greater than or equal to the price. This individual self-interest was seen to lead to equilibrium market price and output levels at which marginal cost equals marginal benefit—moreover, given tastes and technology, government cannot improve on these output levels.

But suppose a buyer, in consuming a good, has a negative impact on other people (e.g., trips leading to congestion, noise pollution from stereos, or smoke from a fireplace). This case is depicted in figure 4.1, where beginning at a fairly low output level others begin to be harmed by increasing consumption of the goods generating the negative externalities.

The negative benefits that others receive—the congestion, the air pollution, or the noise pollution—subtract from the private benefits to arrive at the full marginal social benefits of consuming goods with negative consumption externalities. Hence, the true social benefits of consuming such goods lie below the private benefits as shown by the dashed line in figure 4.1. In the uncontrolled case, consumers would take too many trips, light too many fires, and play stereos too loud. The equilibrium quantities of activities giving rise to negative externalities is too large, at Q_E, relative to the socially optimal quantities, shown as Q^* in the figure. The welfare loss from too much of the offending activity is the (generally growing) sum of the amounts by which marginal cost exceeds marginal benefits for output between Q^* and Q_E. This welfare loss is shown by the shaded area in figure 4.1.

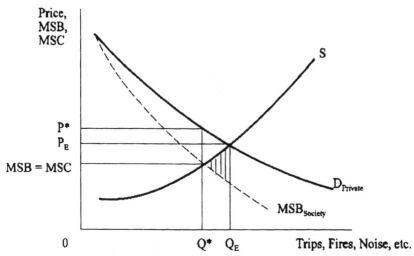

Figure 4.1. The case of a good with negative consumption externalities

It should be noted that the external damages to those harmed actually fall by a larger amount than the shaded area, when moving from Q_E to Q^*. The external harm is reduced by the entire area above the $MSB_{Society}$ curve but below the $D_{Private}$ curve between Q^* and Q_E. The environmental gain, in excess of the shaded area, is a transfer from those who consume the good that gives rise to the negative external effects to those experiencing them.

Where is the missing market here? The missing market stems from the fact that the negative impacts on those harmed do not register with those engaging in activities giving rise to those negative impacts. An obvious way to correct this situation, first advanced by Arthur Pigou in 1920,[1] is to increase the price (by a "tax" or "fine"[2]) on those consuming the good in an amount equal to the marginal damages they impose on those harmed.[3] If a tax is charged in an amount equal to the vertical distance between $D_{Private}$ and $MSB_{Society}$, those consuming the damaging good will face a full price of P^*, which will result in Q^* of the offending activity being chosen. This tax will replace the missing market, returning society to the desirable efficiency results of the perfect market case. That is, the good will be valued by society at an amount that *includes* any remaining environmental damages.

What if the external impacts on society are *positive*? There are many examples of such cases. While employing long-lasting pesticides to eliminate aphids from your rosebushes may result in negative externalities to those breathing air or drinking water (as depicted in figure 4.1), using ladybugs for that purpose results in positive externalities—some of the bugs will migrate to neighboring properties and chomp on aphids there, conferring external benefits. Perhaps the most important example of positive externalities is provided by years of education. There is considerable evidence that those with more education are less likely to be unemployed or commit violent crimes; moreover, they are unlikely to fully capture the full social value of any inventions or innovations they create. And, by obtaining greater education they just become more interesting to talk to at social gatherings and elsewhere.

The case of positive consumption externalities is depicted in figure 4.2. In this case private benefits do not fully capture all of the benefits of consuming the good in question, education or ladybugs, in the figure. Adding the external benefits to the private benefits yields the curve labeled MB_{Social} which is, on efficiency grounds, the social benefits that must be compared to social costs to arrive at the best levels of production and exchange. In the case of positive externalities, the uncontrolled equilibrium will result in underproduction of the good in question, because self-interested buyers have no incentive to consider benefits that they do not receive. In figure 4.2 this is reflected by Q_E falling short of Q^*, with a welfare loss from failure to produce and exchange more of the good depicted by the shaded area. The seemingly obvious policy implication, again due to Pigou, is to subsidize the buyer of the good, providing an incentive to purchase more. If, as is ideal, the subsidy were set equal to the size of the marginal external benefit, buyers would have an incentive to purchase Q^*, the socially optimal quantity of the good.[4]

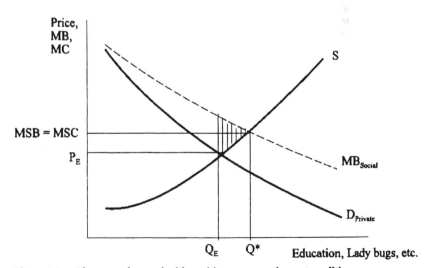

Figure 4.2. **The case of a good with positive consumption externalities**

The preceding cases have been presented largely to become familiar with the full range of situations in which buyers face prices—which provide information and incentives to act on that information—that are "wrong," either being too high or too low. Prices are too low when buyers confer negative impacts on others by their decisions to buy that they have no incentive to consider (a missing market). Prices are too high when buyers confer positive benefits on others by their decisions to buy, again a missing market, because those benefits are not reflected in the incentives facing the buyer.

A particularly relevant situation for environmental economists and environmentalists is that of negative externalities stemming from producer behavior (e.g., air or water pollution, CO_2 buildup, hazardous substance releases, and so on).[5] Here the missing market is clear, in that the producer pays a zero price for a scarce good. Consider the case of steel production. Steel producers must pay for their materials (forms of iron ore and coal), for capital (blast furnaces), and for their labor. Indeed, they must pay the going competitive prices for these inputs, and those prices will represent the opportunity costs of the inputs—they must pay what those inputs could have earned elsewhere, or they will not be able to acquire them. But in producing steel, one input into production is the air that goes into the blast furnaces clean and comes out dirty. In the uncontrolled case, the steel company does not have to pay this cost to society of producing steel—the missing market.

In figure 4.3 this case is depicted. The private marginal costs *that the steel company must pay* comprise the supply curve, $S = MC_{Private}$, as usual. The private marginal benefits to steel buyers are shown as the ordinary demand curve, $D = MB$. When the costs to society associated with the diminished air quality are added to the private production costs, we arrive at the true marginal social costs of production, the dashed curve labeled MC_{Social} in figure 4.3. The external social costs (the negative externalities) associated with steel production are shown as being zero for low levels of steel production but rising more steeply, reflecting increasing marginal damages as is reasonable.

Delving more deeply into figure 4.3, we see that steel producers will produce too much steel without regulation—at Q_E the true marginal cost of the last unit of steel produced is far in excess of the marginal benefit. The shaded area in the figure shows the welfare loss from too much steel, relative to the optimal level of steel production, Q^*, at which the full marginal social costs of steel production are paid.

Again, it is noteworthy that the environmental improvement is substantially larger than the welfare gain in going from Q_E to Q^*. The improvement in environmental quality is the entire area under the MC_{Social} curve and above the $S = MC_{Private}$ curve between Q_E and Q^*.

However, it is also the case that there are, at the economist's social optimum, remaining damages—the area below the MC_{Social} curve and above the

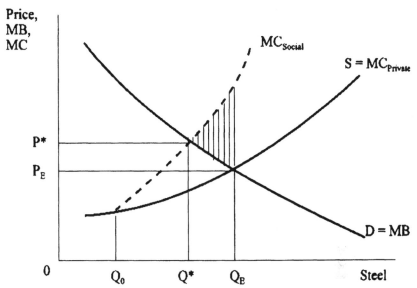

Figure 4.3.   The case of a good with negative production externalities

$S = MC_{Private}$ curve between Q_0 (where environmental damage begins to occur) and Q^*. From the perspective of making human beings as well off as possible these remaining environmental damages are worth it, in the sense that the goods obtained have benefits to society greater than costs, both private and environmental.

In this chapter we have seen that the invisible hand described in chapter 2 will fail to provide the right amounts of goods in the presence of externalities. Two situations are of concern to environmentalists. First, when sellers do not pay the full marginal social costs of production, they will oversupply goods resulting in pollution levels that are too large. Second, when buyers confer negative benefits on other households, they will overdemand goods, resulting in pollution levels that are too large. From the perspective of economists, then, environmental problems are synonymous with negative externalities.

It should be again reiterated that at the economists' optimum, there will generally continue to be remaining environmental damages, and those damages might be viewed as being of great importance to environmentalists. The stance taken throughout this book is, however, that we—the economists—are systematically understating the external damages associated with production and consumption of goods and services. A reasonable question to begin asking is, "If we accurately internalized all externalities facing humans, how undesirable would remaining environmental damages be from anyone's perspective?"

We turn, in chapter 5, to an alternative, or perhaps supplementary, way of thinking about environmental problems. Because externalities would be expected to largely occur in public good media, such as air or water, properly internalizing such externalities would result in optimal levels of air or water quality. Conversely, optimal levels of air or water quality—when marginal benefits equal marginal costs—will be achieved only when we have fully internalized all externalities. Environmental public goods are, however, a subset of the broader class of public goods that we seek to understand in the following chapter.

QUESTIONS FOR DISCUSSION

1. Figure 4.1 could have been thought about in a different way, arguing that the full social costs are greater than the private costs, rather than the full social benefits are less than the private benefits. Graph this way of thinking about negative consumption externalities. Does how one chooses to look at it make any difference? Is one approach more natural for you than the other?
2. What area in figure 4.1 represents the amount of environmental damage at Q_E that is non-optimally large? Why is that area larger than the area of welfare loss to society as a whole from being at Q_E?
3. Is it possible an environmental problem as seen by an environmentalist might be not be seen as an environmental problem by an economist? (Hint: Are there negative externalities that have no biological consequences, hence might not concern environmentalists? Are there activities with biological consequences that might not result in negative externalities?)

NOTES

1. A. C. Pigou, *The Economics of Welfare*, 4th ed. (London: Macmillan and Co., 1934).
2. Fines are usually more popular with environmentalists, because they convey disapproval of the activity under consideration. However, if the fine is set higher than marginal damages, society collectively will be made *worse* off because a smaller than optimal amount of the offending activity will occur. Economists, it should be emphasized, care about society *as a whole*, which includes the preferences of those damaging as well as those damaged.
3. It turns out that whether this tax is actually turned over to compensate those harmed, as many might feel fair, is largely a matter of equity—the critical thing is that those doing the damage face the full marginal cost of their activities, including marginal damages.

4. The subsidy would shift the apparent marginal cost curve, S, downward until it intersects the demand curve at Q^*.

5. While much emphasis is typically placed on producers, large quantities of pollution emanate from the household sector (e.g., automobile pollution, much water pollution, much CO_2 buildup, fireplace pollution, solid waste generation, and noise, among many other pollution categories). Also, while it is possible that producers could confer external benefits on society (perhaps pleasant smells emanating from a potato chip factory), such cases are rare.

5

Public Goods as Missing Markets

The previous chapter considered positive and negative externalities as one type of situation in which missing markets result in nonoptimal levels of private goods production and consumption. In this chapter, we consider a case in which missing markets result in nonoptimal levels of a *public good*—it turns out that the two cases are frequently related.

First, we must know what is meant by a public good. A good is not defined as a public good just because it is provided publicly. A school lunch, for example, is a private good regardless of whether the parents send their students to school with their lunches or whether the lunches are provided publicly (funded with higher tax payments) by the school. It is the case, however, that public goods must generally be provided publicly, because, as we shall see, their nature makes them unprofitable to provide privately.

A *pure public good* is defined by two traits, both critical to its definition. For a good to be a pure public good it must be both *nonrivalrous in consumption* and *nonexcludable in consumption*. A private good, say a hamburger or t-shirt, is rivalrous in the sense that if you eat the hamburger or wear the t-shirt, nobody else can. A good is nonrivalrous in consumption if any individual's consumption of the good does not affect the ability of others to consume the good.

For example, the light from a lighthouse has the property that if you look at it to avoid the dangerous rocks, it does not diminish the ability of anyone else to receive the same benefit. National defense, a court system, the radio and television airwaves, global positioning signals, and other goods share this property. Examples for environmentalists would be species preservation (if the species is saved, the benefits you receive do not reduce the benefits I receive) or CO_2 abatement (your consumption of a less-warm earth does not diminish my ability to enjoy the benefits from a less-warm earth).[1]

But the second trait defining pure public goods is equally critical to understanding their nature. A pure public good must be nonexcludable in consumption. For ordinary private goods, the customer must pay for the good or they are unable to acquire it, for example the hamburger or t-shirt already mentioned. Consider again, however, the light from the lighthouse. If the lighthouse gets built and operating, it is not possible to exclude anybody from benefiting from the light. If the species gets saved you cannot be prevented from receiving the benefits you associate with saving that species.

The non-excludability of pure public goods is the trait that is critical to why such goods are not profitable to supply privately. Suppose, for example, that you were considering building a large air filtration system that would not only clean up your air but also many hundreds or thousands of peoples' air downwind from you. So, you approach them asking for donations to help pay for the expensive contraption that will benefit everyone. Each household you approach will realize two things: a) it is too small to make a difference on whether the contraption actually gets built or not, and b) if the contraption *does* get built it cannot be excluded from receiving the benefits whether it pays or not.

Another example: Someone knocks on your door and asks you to contribute toward saving the blue whale from extinction. You might *say* "Sorry, but you caught me at a really bad time. . . . I have tuition to pay and school books to buy and my rent has gone up." But you also know that the whale is either going to get saved or it is not, and the amount that you would truly be willing to pay to save it (say $10) will have a negligible impact on the outcome. Whether the whale gets saved depends on what the other 120 million households do—if they each give $10, which adds up to $1.2 billion dollars, then the whale just might get saved. But the odds of *your* $10 being decisive are vanishingly small. So, if you keep your $10, you can go buy two pitchers of beer to toast to the saving of the whale (if it gets saved), or you can go buy two pitchers of beer, sadly toasting to the demise of the whale (if it does not get saved). You have an incentive to be a "free rider," and you are just like everybody else. Because everyone has an incentive to free ride, the ride does not exist—the whale goes extinct.

So we have another case of a missing market, depicted for the case of public goods in figure 5.1. But unlike the case of externalities discussed in the previous chapter, in this case the market for saving whales or cleaning up the air *does not exist at all*. No suppliers enter the market, because they cannot get demanders to pay them for something they cannot be excluded from receiving for free. Hence, in figure 5.1 zero is produced instead of Q* (the level of the public good that equates marginal benefits and marginal costs).

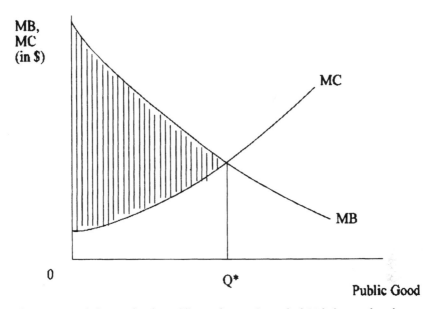

Figure 5.1. Missing market for public goods, zero instead of Q* being produced

The private sector will not produce public goods, so the public sector will have to produce them, if we are to consume the mix of private and public goods that we desire, the mix that gives us maximum welfare given our preferences. Note, however, that figure 5.1 is drawn as *if* we really knew where the marginal benefit and marginal cost curves are located. If we actually did have that information, it would be a trivial matter for the government to produce the optimal, Q*, level of the public good. But, of course, we do not know the position or slope of either curve in figure 5.1 (though the marginal cost curve is viewed as being much easier to pin down). Much of the rest of this book is about how economists attempt to ascertain where the MB curve is in figure 5.1. If we think it is further to the left than it really is, we will underproduce the public good; if we think it is further to the right than it really is, we will overproduce the public good. For reasons presented throughout the remainder of this book, the former situation—underprovision of public goods—is far more likely to occur in practice.

It should be emphasized that aggregating from individual preferences for the public good to the market demand curve (the MB curve in figure 5.1) works differently from how individual preferences were aggregated for ordinary private goods when aggregating from individual to market demand. The appropriate question in the case of ordinary private goods is "How many hamburgers will be demanded at $3.00?" "How many at $2.00?"

These hypothetical questions are asked for all possible prices, and market demands are the sum of individual demands. That is, we add up individual demands *horizontally* to find out how many hamburgers will be demanded at various prices and compare that to the number of hamburgers that will be supplied at those prices. If the aggregate quantities demanded equal the aggregate quantities supplied, the price is in equilibrium . . . otherwise it will either rise (if quantity demanded exceeds quantity supplied) or fall (if quantity supplied exceeds quantity demanded) as discussed in chapter 2.

For public goods we add individual demands *vertically*, not horizontally. That is, the appropriate question now becomes "How much will people collectively value a one unit increase in the public good?" That this is the appropriate question stems from the fact that if a one unit increase in the good takes place, we all get to consume that increase. If we clean up the air, the benefits of the sick and rich (which might be high) will be added to the benefits of the poor and healthy (which would be lower) to get an aggregate benefit. If that aggregate benefit exceeds the marginal cost of providing the one unit increase, on the grounds of efficiency, society will be better off collectively if the unit is produced. As long as the vertically aggregated marginal benefits exceed the marginal provision cost, we are collectively better off continuing to increase the public good (to the level Q^* in figure 5.1). If we really knew where the MB and MC curves were in figure 5.1, the quantity of the public good that we would choose to produce would be *exactly* analogous to a perfectly functioning private market. We would, in this case, have the right amounts of all goods private and public.

So far, we have talked only about *pure* public goods, goods having both of the properties of non-rivalry and non-excludability. But it is possible to have any combination of rivalrous/nonrivalrous and excludability/non-excludability. While private goods, that are both rivalrous and excludable, and pure public goods, that are both nonrivalrous and nonexcludable, are extreme cases, some intermediate cases are of great importance to environmentalists.

For a case of non-rivalry but excludability consider, up to the point of congestion, rides at an amusement park. The rides are nonrivalrous—Andrew consuming a ride does not diminish the ability of Barbara to take a ride. But access to the park is controlled by the owner with fences and gates where entrance fees are collected; hence individuals can be excluded from the nonrivalrous good by the provider. The providers of such goods generally charge a fixed entrance fee and then a zero charge for each ride, controlling congestion by how many people they let into the park. Such goods are profitable to provide by entrepreneurs, and it is unlikely that there are any significant misallocations of resources in this case. Environmental examples might include eco-tours to visit the mountain gorillas of Rwanda or Congo, for which a fee must be paid.

The more important case from the environmentalist's perspective is the case where the good is rivalrous but nonexcludable, the so-called "tragedy of the commons."[2] For pure public goods recall that there was no harm to anyone else from your consumption of the good (the marginal cost is zero, because everyone else can consume as much as they want regardless of how much you consume). And, even for private goods—in the absence of externalities—decisions reached individually will also be the best for society (Adam Smith's well-known point about the invisible hand). But for many goods there is a small harm to others that grows, sometimes greatly, as more people consume the good; in this case best individual decisions might not lead to best collective decisions.

Consider the commons, a communal area of land not privately owned, where cattle, sheep, and the like can roam at will. A rational herdsman will look at *his* marginal benefits and marginal costs of adding another cow to his herd. The marginal animal will have high benefits to the herdsman, but the deterioration of the commons resulting from overgrazing associated with his specific marginal animal will appear as a small cost to *him*, though the aggregate harm from all herders together might be large. But each herdsman has an incentive to think the same way, and the common area is destroyed as the population of herdsman and cattle expand.

Consider another example of a case, the case of prairie dogs that is akin to the tragedy of the commons in spirit. While the herdsman receives benefits that result in collective destruction of the commons, the rancher or farmer with prairie dogs incurs costs that result in the collective destruction of the prairie dog. In some abstract sense, we all like prairie dogs; they are cute, furry, and sociable creatures. But to an individual farmer or rancher prairie dogs will generally have costs greater than their cuteness benefits. To the farmer, prairie dogs are a scourge, denuding the land of valuable vegetation, creating holes for livestock to break their legs in, having fleas that might carry bubonic plague, and so on. As a consequence, many such farmers or ranchers may want to eliminate prairie dogs from their land, despite the small amount of personal affection they might also feel for the critters. However, the behavior of each individual farmer results in a collective outcome that is viewed as undesirable to society as a whole, because prairie dogs can be driven to extinction by the farmers and ranchers taken as a whole.

The problem is, of course, much more general than the herdsman or prairie dog case (e.g., taking a trip at rush hour results in a large social cost on others taking trips or a fire in a fireplace damages many people a small amount). Such cases return us to the externality problem discussed previously. However, recognizing that external damages tend to occur in common areas not privately owned (e.g., congestion in national parks, pollution in air or water, or traffic congestion), provides a potential solution to environmental problems, to be taken up in the next chapter.

The preceding also clarifies the mysterious comment at the outset of this chapter that public goods and externalities are frequently related; externalities tend to occur in public good media. That is, it is much more likely that someone will put a log on the fire damaging your air than it is that they will dump trash over the fence on your land. The reason is that your land has clearly defined property rights, while it is difficult to know—even conceptually—what air is yours. We shall return to property rights as a solution to environmental problems in the next chapter. For now, the example of this paragraph can be taken as preliminary evidence that clearly defined property rights (e.g., for land but not necessarily for air) might be one reason why we have fewer environmental problems than we would otherwise have.

The policy implications of the material on public goods in this chapter are that we would like to provide public goods in a way that is exactly analogous to private goods provision. That exact analogy, for *pure* public goods would be to add up vertically what an increment to the public good is worth to arrive at aggregate marginal benefits (because we each benefit from the increment) and compare those benefits with marginal provision costs. This was depicted in figure 5.1.

For cases of *impure* public goods (goods that are either nonexcludable or nonrivalrous but not both), we would want decision makers to act on true social marginal costs and social marginal benefits when those differ from individually perceived marginal costs and benefits. In the tragedy of the commons example, efficiency requires that the herdsman be charged the marginal cost to *all* herdsmen for a marginal cow. Such a charge would greatly exceed the congestion harm to the herdsman *herself* or *himself* for adding another cow to the herd, assuming there are many herdsmen.[3] Similarly, those throwing another log on the fire should be charged, not just for the cost of the log, but also for the aggregate damage to everyone whose air is worsened as a result of the burning of that log. And in deciding whether to take a trip during rush hour, each individual driver should, on efficiency grounds, be charged an amount that incorporates how much all drivers are damaged by that trip. Such cases were discussed more completely in the previous chapter, while here we are pointing out that external damages tend to occur in impure public goods media.

One might argue, "Wow, don't we already pay enough in taxes and fees . . . won't this just increase everyone's cost of living?" But such taxes can be made revenue neutral by lowering other taxes that we pay (e.g., income taxes). So we could have more optimal amounts of all goods (e.g., faster commutes, more saved species, or optimally used commons) while reducing labor supply distorting income taxes.[4]

There are some important equity issues that have not received sufficient attention, equity issues for public goods that are not present, in quite the same way, for ordinary private goods. The wrinkle of concern is that a public good might be efficient to provide (have overall benefits greater than provision costs), yet might have benefits far less than costs for groups that we care about. Illustrating, suppose a coastal resort town in California is considering building a lighthouse to guide boaters away from some nearby dangerous rocks; who is likely to benefit most from the light, the rich or the poor? The poor are unlikely to have boats at all, and any boats they might have would be of lower value than the pricey yachts of the rich; moreover, the rich might be willing to pay more for safety than the poor.

Suppose, for concreteness, that each of 500 poor households would value the lighthouse at $0.50 per year, the positive value perhaps stemming from greater ability to obtain one's bearings even on land. The 4,000 middle-class households might value the lighthouse at $6.00 per year, having small boats and being a bit risk averse. The rich, perhaps another 500 households value the lighthouse at $90.00 per year. If the lighthouse is built, each group receives their benefits, and indeed cannot be prevented from receiving their benefits. Those benefits come to $250 for the poor, $24,000 for the middle class, and $45,000 for the rich per year of the lighthouse's operation. Suppose all operating and capital costs for the lighthouse come to $50,000 per year.

Should the lighthouse be constructed on efficiency grounds? Yes, because the benefits are $250 + $24,000 + $45,000 = $69,250 per year, and the costs are only $50,000 per year. Society is collectively better off by $19,250 if the lighthouse is constructed. But this does not mean that *each individual household* is better off if the lighthouse is constructed. Whether that is the case or not depends on how the lighthouse is financed.

There are many ways that the lighthouse being considered could be financed. It could be funded by a special assessment on each household in the resort town, in this case $10.00 per household per year (because we have assumed there are 5,000 households, and the lighthouse costs $50,000 per year). Suppose the decision to have the lighthouse was put to a referendum with such a special assessment . . . how would the vote go? Clearly, the lighthouse would be voted down in a landslide victory for the anti-lighthouse voters. Why? Because the lighthouse is only worth $0.50 to the poor and $6.00 per year to the middle class, yet both groups would be required to pay $10.00 per year. Only the 500 rich households would vote for the lighthouse, so the referendum would fail by a huge margin of 4,500 no votes to a mere 500 yes votes.

Similar results would be likely to occur if the lighthouse were to be financed by an increase in the sales or income tax rate. Yet the benefits outweigh the costs, so there ought to be *some* financing scheme that would work. In the present example, perhaps a boat tax based on boat value could be employed. In this case, the (boatless) poor would not have to pay, while the boats of the middle class might be taxed $3.00 per year. This would bring in revenue of $12,000 per year (zero from the poor and $3 times 4,000 middle class households), leaving only $38,000 to come from the rich, which comes to $76.00 per rich household. With this financing scheme, the vote would now be *unanimous* in favor of the lighthouse, because every individual household—poor, middle class, or rich—would experience positive net benefits (aggregate benefits greater than construction costs) from the lighthouse.

There will, at least in principle, always be some financing scheme that can make any project with overall benefits exceeding costs politically palatable. However, such schemes can sometimes be quite complicated, and moreover, may be unnecessary. Here is why: As long as there are no *systematic* biases against any particular group, doing all public good projects when benefits exceed or equal costs will *on average* make us better off than if we do not pursue such projects.

Clarifying, there are many projects (e.g., housing aid, food stamps) that help the poor, others (e.g., home loan interest tax deductions) help the middle class, and still others help the rich (e.g., rapid oil depletion allowances). Moreover, progressive income taxation also contributes toward a fairer average spending/tax outcome. It might not be critical, then, to worry about the equity implications of every single potential project, particularly the small ones that will not have a large equity impact. One must remember, too, that efficient projects increase wealth, because they have benefits greater than costs (raise the value of our scarce resources).

Unlike the case with private goods, much of the preceding equity difficulties stem from the fact that we cannot *individually* choose how much of a public good to get. For a private good, if you really like it, you buy a lot; if you really dislike it, nobody forces you to buy it. But, in the case of a public good, we get what is collectively supplied, neither more nor less, regardless of how much we individually want. Unfortunately, for some households, provision levels will be too low, while—equally unfortunately—for others provision levels will be too high. Moreover, the closer we are to a true optimal amount, the greater is the amount of disagreement about whether we have the right amount. If we have far too little relative to typical desires (e.g., air quality in 1970), there will be great unanimity in pleas for more, while if we have extremely stringent standards there might be widespread calls to relax them. But, the closer we are to the right amount the more likely it is that about half the people will think it is too much and about half will think it is too little. This is a problem without a solution, but it should be borne in mind when observing debate about environmental quality and other public goods.

In this chapter, we have described a theoretical way of thinking about public goods, which is exactly analogous to private goods provision. Suppose we *could* observe individual values for a public good like we can for private goods (buying a private good reveals that it is worth at least what it costs, and we have an incentive to keep buying until it is worth exactly what it costs). Then we would just add those values up (vertically, because we all get the good, if it comes into existence), and compare that sum to the cost of providing it.

The problem, as emphasized in this chapter, is that people have no incentive to accurately reveal what a good is worth to them, which makes the government's task quite difficult. This difficulty, along with many others that stem from it, will provide grist for most of the rest of the book. Before turning to how to find out what the marginal benefits of a public good are, we turn to an alternative approach: trying to figure out how to turn public goods into private goods, so we do not have to face these valuation difficulties.

QUESTIONS FOR DISCUSSION

1. How common do you think public goods are? Attempt to think of as many examples as possible.
2. Why are public goods nonprofitable for the private sector to produce?
3. Why was it argued that marginal benefits (marginal willingness to pay) should be added *vertically* for public goods and what does that mean?
4. Why is the case of public goods referred to as another example of a missing market?
5. Do you think that many public goods are so-called merit goods? Should people desire such goods more than they actually do? If government decision makers were to take this position, would they make people better off or worse off as the people themselves saw it?
6. Give as many examples as you can conjure up of goods that lie between ordinary private goods and pure public goods.
7. Do you think that a good that is excludable but nonrivalrous will always be provided optimally by the private sector? Should amusement parks charge a fixed admission with a zero dollar price for each ride? Or should they let people in free and charge them for each ride? What would that decision depend on from the perspective of the decision maker? From the perceptive of society?
8. Do you believe that there *is* or is *not* a systematic bias against certain groups in society? The text only discussed bias in terms of favoring or disfavoring certain income groups—what other groups might one care about?

NOTES

1. It should perhaps be noted at this point that, depending on provision level, a public good for one person can be a public bad for another. For example, some people feel that we have too much national defense while others think we have too little. In the global warming case, a person in Siberia might benefit from global warming while a person in Bangladesh might be harmed. In *most* of the contexts we will be focusing on, this distinction will not be critical to understanding.

2. See Garrett Hardin, "The Tragedy of the Commons," *Science* 162 (1968): 1243–48.

3. Note that the tragedy of the commons disappears if there is only one herdsman, because all congestion costs are internalized; the herdsman's marginal private costs will be, in this case, the marginal social costs.

4. While beyond the scope of this text, keeping environmental taxes and fees revenue neutral by cutting distortionary taxes (e.g., income taxes) is sometimes said to result in a double dividend from those environmental taxes. They make us collectively better off not only because we get a more optimal amount of environmental goods, but also because we have a more optimal labor market outcome, because labor supply decisions are less distorted by the income tax.

6

Property Rights as a Potential Solution to Environmental Problems

Where would you more expect to see graffiti, in a public restroom or in the bathroom of a private home? Would you expect to find a condominium and its surroundings that are occupied by an owner, all other things being equal, to be in better or worse shape than a condominium that is occupied by a renter? Are you more likely to check the oil of a rental car or of a car you own? Which are more likely to go extinct, cows and chickens or rhinos and elephants? Are you more likely to save (for future consumption) fish in the ocean that you do not own (and anyone can catch) or fish in your pond that you *do* own? In all such cases, why? The answer, while not equally obvious in all cases, is one that we shall study and is that *owned* resources will be better cared for because of the incentives that property rights confer on the owners.

If you own something you are obviously wealthier than if you do not own that thing. But more important for present purposes, you *care* about the things that you own and attempt to take any action with benefits—to you—greater than costs—to you—to maintain them.

Consider, for example, the simple case of an ordinary private home with a value of $300,000. This home can either be maintained or not maintained. If it is maintained, it will hold its value, but if it goes unmaintained it will fall in value; that is, it will depreciate.[1] Suppose some act of maintenance, say painting the exterior, costs $2,000. Will that maintenance take place? If the house would fall in value to $296,000 without the paint job, yes, the maintenance would be expected to occur. This is because the owner will be $2,000 worse off by failing to paint (saving the $2,000 paint job but having his house fall in value by $4,000). Generally one would expect rational people to take care of the things they own because failing to do so

75

will lower their wealth, hence their future consumption of the things they care about.

Turning to one of the more explicitly environmental examples mentioned previously, would you expect whales, elephants, or ocean fish to be more or less likely to go extinct than cows, chickens, or pigs? The key to understanding this, and many other resource allocation questions in this chapter, is the role of property rights in the incentives that face decision makers. And as emphasized throughout this book, the failure to have effective property rights creates another type of missing market, and missing markets always lead to resource misallocation.

It should be clear that it is not the greed of mankind that leads to endangered species, because our greed applies equally to cows and whales, pigs and elephants, or chickens and ocean fish. What is the distinguishing—truly important—difference? Cows, pigs, and chickens are *owned*, and whales, elephants, and ocean fish are (generally) unowned. This is partly a technological matter of what species are easiest to own; it is quite difficult to own a whale or elephant, because the former must forage over vast ocean areas, and the latter is difficult to pen in. Some things are easier to own than others, and as a result some things have been owned for so long that we have forgotten the great importance of the distinction between owning and not owning.

Ronald Coase won the Nobel Prize in economics in 1991, in large part for what later became known as the Coase theorem. In some ways, the Coase theorem is simple . . . it is really merely supply and demand in a different guise. In the case of ordinary supply and demand, you own your own labor and you can buy various goods, obtaining property rights to them. Sellers can only sell things to you that they wish to and that they themselves have property rights to that are transferable.

What are property rights? They are the rights possessed by the owner of any good or resource. When you buy a car, for example, you have the rights that come with that purchase, but you do not have the right to kill people with your car or drive on the sidewalks to avoid traffic jams, and so on. Property rights might be thought of as a bundle of sticks associated with ownership; if the right to drive on either side of the road is eliminated by a law requiring drivers to stay on the right side (as in the United States) or on the left side (as in the United Kingdom), a stick of freedom has been removed from your bundle. Of course, the removal of that stick might have benefits far exceeding costs, for such a law greatly increases the probability of arriving safely at any destination, but it is a restriction on *individual* freedom nonetheless.

So what is the Coase theorem? There are many ways to express it, but a version explicitly oriented toward environmentalists is as follows:

Under certain circumstances (if property rights are clearly defined and if transactions costs are sufficiently small), the efficient outcome will occur (cleaning up the environment if benefits are greater than costs and not cleaning up the environment if costs are greater than benefits), regardless of who is assigned rights in the environment. This will occur automatically and does not require intervention by government.

The theorem is important to environmentalists, regardless of whether the (somewhat restrictive) circumstances are met or not. If the circumstances are met, we shall see that externalities become *self-internalizing* via the legal system. One way to think about the Coase theorem is that it is the reason that we do not have *more* environmental problems than we do. Illustrating, a neighbor is much less likely to dump his or her garbage over a fence separating your backyards than to have a fire in his or her fireplace—why? Both activities damage you, perhaps even by equal amounts, but it is rare that trash is dumped over your fence and common to observe fires in fireplaces. The critical difference in these cases relates to transactions costs.

Transactions costs are the costs that need to be incurred to facilitate a transaction. Some transactions have low costs associated with them, such as buying ordinary frequently purchased goods. Other transactions, like the purchase of a house and to a lesser extent a used car, involve much larger transaction costs. This is one of the reasons that such purchases occur infrequently.

In most environmental cases, the cause of high transactions costs are usually that there are a large *number* of people damaged—each being damaged a small amount—by numerous firms. In such cases, individual pollution damages might be small relative to the costs of attempting to negotiate a better outcome, even when pollution can be cleaned up quite cheaply. It is also difficult to know how much pollution is attributable to any particular polluter. As a practical matter, the number of individuals and firms usually has to be somewhat small for Coase's theorem to be applicable.

The easiest way to understand the Coase theorem and its implications is to go over a number of examples that clarify how it works. We will consider three cases: the draft systems used in various professional sports, a case of air pollution, and a water allocation example.

THE PROFESSIONAL SPORTS DRAFT

It is commonly argued that allowing professional teams with the worst records to have priority in the drafting of collegiate athletes results in greater parity in the professional leagues, making games closer hence more exciting. The Coase theorem suggests that this is not true. It argues instead that each athlete will go to the team that places the highest value on that player regardless of draft order. In other words, the efficient outcome will occur, regardless of the property rights assignment given by the draft. It is certainly the case that many trades involving players, draft picks, and money routinely take place—what motivates those trades?

Consider Ben Pillpoppin, a power hitter and this year's likely number one draft pick in baseball. Everyone expects Ben to be drafted by the New York Mets, the team with the worst record in professional baseball. Suppose Ben is worth $4 million to the Mets, and he agrees to play for them for $3 million.[2] Suppose further that Ben is worth $6 million to the Yankees, maybe because *everybody* is worth more to the Yankees (e.g., greater game day attendance, more valuable TV rights, and so on) or perhaps because the Yankees have a greater relative need (demand) for a slugger. Will Ben stay with the Mets?

No, it is not in the interest of the Mets to keep Ben. There will be a voluntary transaction making both the Mets and the Yankees better off that sends Ben to the Yankees. There is some amount between $4 million and $6 million, say $5 million for simplicity, which will make the Mets want to trade Ben to the Yankees. Ben gets his $3 million salary in any case, but the Mets are a million dollars better off by trading him to the Yankees. Similarly, the Yankees are a million dollars better off with Ben, because he is worth $6 million and they only had to pay $5 million for him.

So the draft (who has the property rights in the player) really does not determine who ends up with the various players (they will go to the team that most values them). This is because it is in the *self-interest* of the team owners to make trades that they think will make them better off. In this case, property rights are clearly assigned, because everyone knows the draft order. Moreover, transactions costs are fairly small relative to the potentially large benefits of acquiring or trading away key players.

AIR POLLUTION: THE SMALL NUMBERS CASE

Suppose Steelex Incorporated, a large steel plant, is generating pollution that damages Healthspa, a small resort located downwind from Steelex. For simplicity, assume that Steelex has profits of $2 million per year. The demand for the Healthspa resort is lowered because of the air pollution generated by Steelex. Healthspa would—in the absence of Steelex—have profits of $300,000 but is damaged by $100,000, leaving a profit of $200,000.

We now have four possible cases, summarized in table 6.1. Steelex can be found liable by the courts (that is, Healthspa has the right to experience clean air) and will be required to either discontinue their harm or compensate Healthspa. This case is seen in the left column of table 6.1. After liability is established, there are two subcases with regard to cleanup versus compensation. If the cost of cleanup is small relative to the damages to

Table 6.1. Who Is Liable Does Not Affect the Efficient Outcome

	Steelex liable	Healthspa liable
Costs of cleanup are $50,000	Steelex will clean up, because that is cheaper than compensating Healthspa; B > C of cleanup	Healthspa will offer some amount, say $75,000, to Steelex who will clean up; B > C of cleanup
Costs of cleanup are $150,000	Steelex compensates Healthspa by $100,000, because C > B of cleanup	Cleanup does not occur, and Healthspa continues to receive damage; C > B of cleanup

Healthspa, Steelex will clean up because that is less costly than compensation (e.g., the $50,000 cost of cleanup is less than paying the $100,000 in compensatory damages, the case in the upper left box of the table). If, conversely, the cost of cleanup is large relative to the damages (e.g., the $150,000 of the lower left box), Steelex will compensate Healthspa by the $100,000 of damages rather than clean up. Note that the efficient outcome from society's perspective occurs in this case—Steelex will clean up when the benefits of cleanup (damage reduction) are greater than the costs of cleanup and will not clean up (will compensate for damages) when the costs of cleanup are greater than the benefits.

Perhaps the more startling situation is where Healthspa is found liable for the damages they receive. A court might find that Steelex is not liable for a number of reasons. Steelex might have been in the locality first, and it might be viewed as unfair to penalize them for damages incurred to an entity that moved into the area later. Or a large number of the local citizenry might work for Steelex, and political pressure might result in it not being found liable for damages. What happens in this case? This case is depicted in the right-hand column of table 6.1. In this case Steelex has property rights in the air, being allowed to use as an input clean air and emit as a production by-product dirty air. Again, there are two subcases. Even though Steelex has the right to pollute, if the costs of cleanup are low, Healthspa would be willing to pay some amount, say $75,000, for Steelex to clean up. Doing so makes Healthspa better off (they regain $100,000 of profits by bribing Steelex, for a net gain of $25,000) and also makes Steelex better off (they receive $75,000 for a cleanup effort that only costs $50,000, for a net gain of $25,000).[3]

If, on the other hand, the costs exceed the benefits of cleanup, as in the lower right box of table 6.1, there is no amount that Healthspa would be willing to offer Steelex to clean up that Steelex would be willing to accept. Healthspa is only damaged by $100,000 so would be unwilling to pay more than that to Steelex, and Steelex would not incur $150,000 to clean up unless they are offered at least that much from Healthspa.

Again it should be emphasized that the efficient outcome, from society's perspective, occurs *regardless of the assignment of property rights.* If Steelex is liable they will clean up if that is cheaper than compensating (the compensation is for damages, which are the benefits of cleanup) and will compensate if cleanup costs are greater than damages. If Healthspa is liable (i.e., Steelex is not liable), Steelex will still clean up if cleanup costs are lower than damages, because Healthspa will make it in their interest to do so. But the most Healthspa is willing to pay is the amount of their damage, so if costs of cleanup are larger than that, any offer they might make to Steelex will be turned down as not covering the cost of cleanup.

Some observations need to be made at this point. First, regardless of who has the property rights, their assignment must be clear for the efficient results to occur. Normally, the courts take care of property rights assignment, but in some situations individuals are not aware of who has the property rights. Consider mud splashes from puddles in the road next to sidewalks. Does the car have the right to splash? Or does the pedestrian have the right to not be splashed? In either case, one or the other would be expected to be careful, so the efficient outcome would be expected to occur with minimal conflict. But what if property rights are unclear? If neither the car drivers nor the pedestrians know who has the property rights in mud splashes, they might both assume they have the right, leading to, non-optimally, many splashes.[4]

Second, while it does not matter *to efficiency* who is assigned the property rights, it might matter greatly on *equity* grounds. That is, if households have the right to breathe clean air and must be compensated for any damages, they are wealthier than if they did not have the right to breathe clean air and instead had to purchase the clean air from firms. Similarly, polluting firms are wealthier if they have to be compensated to clean up than if they must either clean up or compensate those damaged. So property rights assignment may be important on equity grounds, despite being unimportant on efficiency grounds.[5] Historically, property rights in air and water pollution were typically at least implicitly assigned to firms. As pollution levels increased with industrial growth, property rights assignment in the use of air and water are increasingly being given to households.

WATER ALLOCATION

Suppose that you are a judge who has to determine the allocation of 100,000 acre feet[6] of water between farmers and ranchers or perhaps between urban and rural users. Who do you give the water to—who, that is, do you assign the property rights to the water? As a judge, you might be concerned about both equity and efficiency. Who is most deserving on grounds of fairness (equity) and who is the highest value user (efficiency)? It turns out, of course, that the Coase theorem indicates that on efficiency grounds *it does not matter to whom you give the water*, as long as water can be voluntarily exchanged among the parties vying for it.[7]

The situation is illustrated in figure 6.1. The horizontal line segment has a length equal to 100,000 acre feet, and any point along that horizontal line represents an allocation. For example, if rural users are assigned all of the water, the allocation is at the left-most end of the line segment (the origin at 0_U for urban users), while if the urban users are allocated all of the water that allocation is depicted at the right-most end of the line segment (the origin at 0_R for rural users). Any other allocation can be represented by any other point along the horizontal line segment, with A* being of particular importance, as we shall see.

On equity grounds, suppose you as the judge feel more sympathetic to the rural users, perhaps because they are poorer or you have a background as a rural person. You will be making the rural users better off by the area under their demand curve for water, seen in the figure as area BF0. But rural users might have relatively low marginal values for water (they can grow more drought-resistant crops or merely suffer some crop loss without the 100,000 acre feet). And, as with all values, the value of extra water gets smaller as more is consumed, with the rural value of water falling to zero at point B, after using perhaps 80,000 of the 100,000 acre feet.

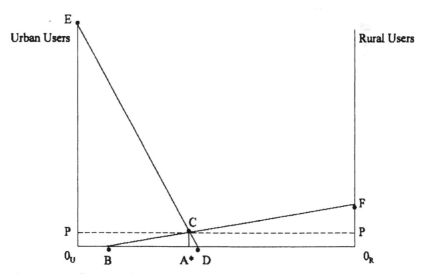

Figure 6.1.   Allocation of 100,000 acre feet of water

Clearly, if the rural users were allowed to sell some water to urban users they would do so. How much would they be willing to sell? Water begins to have a higher marginal value to urban users at A^*. Suppose that A^* represents an allocation of water in which urban users would get 40% (40,000 acre feet) of the water and rural users would get 60% (60,000 acre feet) of the water. If the water is sold to urban users at a price, P, rural users are made much better off—they receive revenue of area $0_U PCA^*$ while only giving up water that was worth the much smaller area BCA^*.[8]

Under Coasian arguments, nothing about the optimal allocation would change were the water initially allocated to the urban users. Suppose you, as the judge, live in an urban area and greatly appreciate the value of being able to flush your toilet and having tap water to drink. The value of the water to urban users might be high for small quantities but might be expected to fall rapidly as the amount of water available is increased. The urban marginal value of the water would come to equal that of rural users at A^* as before, only in this case it is urban users who have the rights to sell water to the rural users. Urban users could receive area A^*CP0_R in dollars of revenue while only losing area A^*CD in dollar value of the water given up.

If society stipulates that water cannot be resold, then the value of the water to society would only be the area under the demand curve of the recipient of the water (either area $BF0_R$ or area $DE0_U$). If, however, the water is given to *either* rural or urban users and allowed to be sold, the allocation will be at A^*, and the value to society of the water will be the entire area under both demand curves up to their intersection (area $0_U ECF0_R$ in the figure).

The Coase arguments are powerful. In the presence of a legal system that assigns property rights and that requires compensation for damages to one's property, externalities *should* be self-internalizing. That is, if you are damaged by a polluter and you have the rights to the clean air, the polluter will either have to compensate you or cease the offending activity. If the polluter has the right to pollute, you can offer some amount (up to the amount you are damaged, because you will not offer more than that) to have the polluter eliminate its marginal damages. So if property rights can be assigned for environmental resources, those resources are likely to be used efficiently, insofar as values are clearly known to the various parties interested in the environmental resources. This approach is certainly worth pursuing in cases where the underlying circumstances (low transactions costs and clearly defined property rights) exist.

There is another advantage—an informational advantage—of the Coase approach to resolution of environmental disputes that is often overlooked. The parties seeking a property rights assignment and either compensation or cessation of the offending activity have an incentive to present their evidence on damages (benefits of cleanup) as persuasively as possible. If a damaged party overstates damages greatly, they might lose credibility. Moreover, the damaging party has an incentive to provide alternative, presumably lower, damage estimates. The actual determination of damages might well be more informed than would be the case if a government bureaucrat with no strong direct interest assigned a pollution tax to internalize the externality.

As we shall see in the next couple of chapters, however, there are reasons to suspect that determining the values to place on environmental damages and resources might be difficult in practice. In particular, we shall see that in many cases individuals have powerful incentives to understate what an environmental resource is worth to society. How can we proceed in such cases?

QUESTIONS FOR DISCUSSION

1. Can you think of additional examples, other than those presented at the opening of this chapter, in which property rights affect resource allocation? For example, are you more likely to repeatedly cut across your own lawn or that of a stranger or your university, in going about your daily activities?

2. The example of the house to be painted might be confusing to some students. One might argue, for example, that the owner might not be able to afford to paint his house, hence might suffer a $4,000 property value loss rather than incur the $2,000 painting expense. Under what circumstances might this argument be valid?

3. All of the text examples of the Coase theorem involved use values, values associated with the use of the player or the air or the water. Suppose there exist a great many people, each with relatively small *nonuse* values, say a value for preservation. Are the assumptions of low transactions costs, necessary for the Coase theorem to have practical relevance, going to be valid in this case? Will the environmental resource be preserved from use or will it be likely to go to the highest valued *use*?

4. Think of other examples in which property rights assignment might be an approach that would lead to efficient resource allocation. Suppose, for example, we privatized our national parks, selling them to the highest bidder. Taxpayers would of course benefit from that revenue, but presumably the winning bidder would change how the parks are operated. What would determine how much the bidder would pay? What equity considerations would matter? Would you expect national parks to be more crowded or less crowded if this policy were enacted? Would entry fees be larger or smaller than at present?

Would you expect any significant amount of waiting in lines to use the environmental resource? Why or why not?

5. What role might bankruptcy play in the arguments presented in this chapter? That is, suppose Steelex is not making profits of $2 million but is near bankruptcy. In this case, property rights assignment might have a large impact. If Steelex has the right to pollute and has to be bribed to reduce pollution, it might stay in business. If Healthspa has the right to clean air and Steelex must either compensate or eliminate the offending activity, Steelex might go out of business. Does this affect the argument?

6. The text examples were mostly of a discrete nature (the player goes to one team or another and the pollution is either eliminated or it is not). How would the Steelex/Healthspa example be modified if the steel company had an increasing marginal cost of cleanup? (Hint: the water allocation example is instructive here, because at A* the marginal values of water are equated).

7. Figure 6.1 was drawn rather unusually vis-à-vis the supply and demand graphs of previous chapters. This was to focus on the allocation of the fixed amount of water between the rural and urban users. How would you depict the situation as an ordinary supply and demand example? What would the equilibrium price and quantity be if the water market were a competitive one? [Hint: the market demand is the horizontal sum of the individual demands, and the supply will be a vertical line at 100,000 acre feet].

NOTES

1. It does not matter whether one substitutes "grow in value" for "hold its value" and "grow more slowly in value" for "fall in value" in this sentence, as will be clear from the text example.

2. Players will not generally be paid what they are worth (the value of their marginal product) until they become free agents. Unless an agreement can be worked out with the team that has their draft rights, they must forgo playing their sport. On becoming a free agent, competitive bidding guarantees that they receive or come close to receiving what they are worth. So despite the apparently huge salaries, drafted players are underpaid.

3. The gains from trade here could be split in any number of ways depending on the bargaining power of the two firms, notions of equity, and so on. But the key insight is that there is some side payment that can make both parties better off whenever the benefits of cleanup exceed the costs of cleanup.

4. In Boulder, Colorado, the pedestrian has the right not to be splashed and can take the car driver that splashes them to small claims court and expect to win damages. This property rights assignment might not be universal, however, as other communities might be more sympathetic to the driver.

5. There could be small so-called wealth effects associated with property rights assignment that have efficiency implications. That is, if households are given the right to breathe clean air (rather than having to pay for it) they are a little bit wealthier than otherwise, and at greater wealth levels they might have higher demands for clean air. Hence the amount of compensation necessary or the size of bribes offered might be affected slightly by who is assigned the property rights.

6. An acre foot is an amount of water that would cover an acre of land (roughly the size of four suburban house lots) to a depth of one foot.

7. Water law in the United States is complicated, differing in different regions of the country and differing greatly among countries. In some cases, voluntary transfers of water between different interested parties is explicitly prohibited, which will be seen as inefficient (and inequitable according to most peoples' values, as well).

8. If there were just one rural user and one urban user, with no markets for water, the price charged by rural owners for some water might be much higher than P, as rural owners would want to take advantage of the high marginal values of urban users for initial quantities. Such so-called price discrimination would alter how much of the benefits of the water go to rural users. They would, however, want to continue to give up marginal amounts of water as long as they received more than it was worth to them. This occurs at price P, which would be the competitive price.

III

IMPORTANT THEORETICAL
PROBLEMS WITH
IMPLEMENTING
BENEFIT-COST ANALYSIS

In this section we discuss two important problems that are really two sides of the same coin. In chapter 5 we discussed public goods that have the unusual properties of being *nonrivalrous* and *nonexcludable*. The fact that such goods are nonrivalrous—that we all get to enjoy any amount that is supplied—argues for adding up everyone's individual marginal values to get the aggregate value to compare to marginal costs. This has been known since at least 1954 when Paul Samuelson wrote a famous paper[1] establishing this methodology as being analogous to perfectly functioning markets for ordinary private goods, goods that are both rivalrous and excludable.

However, Samuelson also noted that it would be difficult in practice to determine individual values because of the non-excludability of such goods, this being the topic we take up in a relatively brief chapter 7. People have an incentive to free ride, hoping to get the good without paying for it—and recognizing, further, that any payment that they might make would have a negligible impact on whether the good is supplied. Attempts to deal with this so-called demand revelation problem have not yet resulted in a methodology with general applicability.

At a pure theoretical level, Samuelson's demand revelation problem also embeds a supply revelation problem, and this problem was only recently recognized explicitly (see Graves, On the Valuation of Pure Public Goods).[2] That is, the traditional discussion of free riding has centered on the difficulty of determining how much individuals are willing to pay out of their income for a public good (or an increment to a public good for continuously variable public goods). Chapter 8 discusses the fact that people can be willing to pay for public goods by giving up ordinary private goods (by spending a portion of their income on them), *or* they can be willing to pay for public goods by giving up leisure (to generate more income to spend on them). Any time there are incentives to free ride out of a given income, there will also be incentives to undergenerate income, as will be seen in detail in chapter 8. This suggests, as a practical matter, that benefit-cost analysis for public goods is being conducted at income levels that are too low, and all of the nongenerated income would have been spent on the public good (apart from so-called general equilibrium effects that are discussed in chapter 8).

Part III, then, argues that it will be difficult to infer what the benefits are for an increment to a public good. Moreover, this part is strongly suggestive that the nature of the revelation problems implies a pronounced undervaluation of public goods. Further the problems extend to any other goods that are collectively determined, regardless of whether such goods are nonrivalrous or nonexcludable.

NOTES

1. P. A. Samuelson, "The Pure Theory of Public Expenditure," *Review of Economics and Statistics* 36 (1954): 387.

2. P. E. Graves, On the Valuation of Pure Public Goods, manuscript, 2006.

7

The Well-Known "Demand Revelation" Problem Out of a Given Income

In chapter 5 public goods were discussed. Such goods have the properties of being nonrivalrous and nonexcludable. Reviewing, non-rivalry means that your consumption of the good does not diminish my ability to consume the good—if it exists, we all get it. That is, if a species is saved or the air gets cleaner, we all benefit. How much we benefit individually depends on how much we care about the species or about air quality. Income and taste variations are large and would generally indicate that our individual benefits would be expected to vary a great deal.

Non-excludability means that if the good exists, nobody can be excluded from enjoying it. If the species is saved or the air gets cleaner, each individual household cannot be kept from enjoying the benefits that brings to the household. Indeed, if any household *could* be kept from enjoying the benefits, they should not be kept from enjoying them, because the marginal social cost of the benefits is zero (because of the nonrivalrous nature of public goods).

But, as also discussed in chapter 5, the non-excludability property of public goods presents a real problem, the focus of this brief chapter and the next. Any rational individual will realize that his or her value for the public good is going to be negligibly small relative to the total value, to the sum of everyone else's values.

The impact of the preceding is that there is an odd missing market situation for public goods. For individuals wishing to *increase* the amount of a public good from its current level (say reduced CO_2 in the atmosphere) the price they face is virtually infinite. Suppose it costs $15 billion dollars to implement a particular policy that resulted in substantial reductions in

CO_2. To virtually any individual (even Bill Gates) this would be effectively infinite, relative to the small individual benefits stemming from the reduction in CO_2. To individuals collectively, the cost would only average $100 per household, assuming 150 million households.

Yet while the price appears to be virtually infinite for increments to the public good, the price is seen by the individual to be effectively zero for whatever happens to be provided (the individual households cannot be excluded from enjoying the good, hence a price cannot be directly charged). To be sure, the levels of the public good that are actually provided must come at a cost that must be paid (there is no such thing as a free lunch for either private or public goods). Real resources must be used to provide the public good, and this will be reflected in either higher prices (e.g., more expensive, but cleaner, cars) or higher taxes (e.g., cleaner municipal water treatment plants). But what is being observed here is the *cost* of whatever is provided (e.g., the $100 per household for carbon dioxide abatement) not the *benefit* associated with increments in the provision level. That is, economists do not know what an increment to the public good is worth, because they cannot observe that. Nobody is buying, individually, the public good, because it is inordinately expensive relative to their individual benefits. And observing the costs of providing an increment to the public good does not provide much direct information about willingness to pay to incur those costs.

So we are in a bind. We cannot look at the sorts of real market behavior we observe for ordinary private goods to infer the marginal value of public goods. People do not buy six-packs of clean air. . . . to any individual cleaning up the air is prohibitively expensive relative to that individual's value, and the individual cannot get other individuals to pay because of the nonexcludability property of public goods. How are we to discover how much individual households value increments to the public good? Without being able to do this, the desirable efficiency features of vertically aggregated marginal willingness to pay as a measure of marginal benefits evaporate. The parallel between perfectly functioning markets for private goods (with horizontal aggregation of individual demands) and perfectly functioning markets for public goods (with vertical aggregation of individual demands) becomes meaningless when we have no information about what we are aggregating. For ordinary private markets, individuals *must* reveal their marginal willingness to pay or they are not able to acquire the good, because they must pay the equilibrium price. We can observe how much is desired at various amounts and estimate a demand curve.

For public goods we have no information to form the basis of the demand curve; individuals do not individually purchase the good, and if it is produced, they have an incentive to lie about what it is worth to them, because they know they will get the good anyway.

In Part IV we discuss the merits and drawbacks of many approaches to inferring what the marginal values are to individuals who have no incentive to reveal them. One might suspect, for example, that if there is a great political clamor for some public good, say environmental quality in the late 1960s and early 1970s, that the benefits might be greater than the costs of a clean air act or other environmental policy. But how do we know how far to go with environmental improvements? Many approaches are discussed in later chapters, but all are seen to be likely to result in undervaluation of environmental goods.

The policy implication of this brief chapter is that any *revealed* demands are likely to be low relative to true demands, because rational individuals will realize they will get whatever is supplied anyway, with any voluntary payment being too small to make a difference in that supply. In the absence of a practical mechanism that creates an incentive for people to accurately reveal their values for environmental and other public goods, might one argue that we should pursue public good projects with *apparent* costs greater than benefits, because benefits are understated?

QUESTIONS FOR DISCUSSION

1. How much of a problem do you feel is created by the incentives to free ride discussed in this chapter and in chapter 5? Might people just reveal, as honestly as possible, what an environmental improvement is worth just by asking them?
2. What would you suspect might be problems with voting on environmental issues? Would the distribution of benefits and costs over the voting population be likely to matter? What about nonvoters?
3. Can you think of any way of using known relationships between ordinary goods and environmental goods to value environmental improvements?

8

A Less-Well-Known "Supply Revelation" Problem

As discussed in chapter 5, for pure public goods, optimal provision levels would result if individual willingness-to-pay were aggregated (added vertically, in a graphical setting) to arrive at marginal benefits to be compared to marginal provision costs. This follows from the nonrivalrous nature of public goods; any individual receiving benefits does not reduce the benefits received by others. Aggregating in this manner should result in levels of public good provision exactly paralleling the desirable efficiency conditions typically associated with perfectly functioning private markets.

As also mentioned in chapter 5 and given greater emphasis in chapter 7, the application of this recommended methodology for optimal public goods provision is problematic in practical policy settings, because the non-excludability property of public goods creates incentives to free ride. Thus, true aggregate marginal willingness to pay is difficult to infer out of a given income, because each individual will have an incentive to understate preferences when asked to contribute. But there is another aspect of the free rider problem, an aspect that has been ignored in the last half century of work on benefit-cost analysis for public goods.

Motivating the discussion of this chapter, consider two types of individuals. The first, Ben Shoppin, desires mega-mansions, expensive sports cars and SUVs, European vacations, designer clothing, gourmet restaurant meals, and fine wine. Ben realizes that he has three options for achieving his goals, only one of which is practical. He could—impractically—hope that someone will give him what he wants or perhaps that he could steal what he wants. Absent philanthropy or theft, however, Ben will realize that the only way to obtain his desired goods is to generate the income necessary to acquire them. The *critical* observation for present purposes, however, is that *if* Ben does generate the income, he can in fact acquire what he wants, because what he wants are ordinary private goods.

Consider now Sten (for strong environmentalist). What Sten desires are more wilderness areas, cleaner air and water, reduced CO_2 buildup, species preservation, and so on. He has quite limited desires for ordinary private goods. Sten differs importantly from Ben, because he will, if rational, realize that any income that he might generate to acquire the public goods that he cares about will be negligible in that collectively determined decision. Because Sten cannot get what he wants by giving up leisure and because leisure is valuable to everyone, Sten will only generate the income necessary to buy the limited range of private goods he desires (and to pay for the costs, in terms of taxes or higher prices, of whatever amount of public goods *are* provided collectively). In extreme cases, Sten and others like him might "drop out" in the jargon of 1960s hippies.[1]

Further clarifying, consider two individuals who are observed to generate fairly low but identical levels of income. One is lazy, placing a high value on leisure and not caring greatly for goods of *any* kind, private or public. The other cares a great deal about public goods of various kinds and other goods that are determined collectively—but he or she recognizes that any income that he or she might generate would have a negligible impact on what he or she cares about. To the economist, these two individuals are *observationally equivalent* in that neither person looks like they have much marginal willingness to pay for *anything*, despite the latter's strong desires for public goods.

As one further example, suppose the link between work effort and work reward were to be broken for ordinary private goods. Imagine, specifically, that an extreme egalitarian communist regime decides that everyone will receive exactly $500 per month of goods and services; they must generate income to pay for those goods and services but cannot acquire more than that quantity, regardless of their income. How much income will a rational worker generate in such a system? Regardless of their true marginal willingness to pay for goods and regardless of how little they might value leisure relative to goods, they will only generate $500 per month of income.

The productivity of the collective farms of the old Soviet Union was low relative to that of the small privately owned farms. Pundits argued at the time that this was because the link between work effort and work reward was broken for the former but not for the latter. But public goods (and goods that cannot be individually incremented more generally) represent an extreme case in which the link between work effort and work reward is fully severed.

In his well-known paper on public goods valuation, Samuelson noted that inputs can be handled just like outputs but with a minus sign preceding them.[2] So at a purely formal level, what is referred to in this chapter as a supply revelation problem is really just a different aspect of the demand revelation problem discussed in the preceding chapter. That is, we all have an endowment of time and money, and we can give up either to get the goods that we want. However, in any situation (e.g., for a pure public good) where it will be difficult to determine individual willingness to pay out of current income because of output market free riding, it will also be difficult to know how much more income would be generated if public goods *could* be purchased as ordinary private goods because of input market free riding.

The implications of the preceding have not been realized by practitioners of benefit-cost analysis for public goods. Specifically, the benefit streams in the numerator are understated, even if demand revelation in output markets were *perfect* out of current income (as discussed in chapter 3, which implicitly made the assumption that we accurately knew the benefits and costs in each period). This follows from the fact that the input market failure to generate income for public goods will remain, because public goods cannot be individually incremented with additional income.

Reiterating, for ordinary private goods one would certainly expect that there would be neither a demand revelation problem nor a supply revelation problem. That is, we must reveal our willingness to pay for the marginal pizza slice or beer to acquire it. Moreover, we also realize that for private goods, barring theft or philanthropy as noted previously, we must generate income by supplying resources—notably labor giving up leisure—to acquire the goods that we desire. Critically, for present purposes, however, we also realize that if we *do* generate income by giving up additional leisure we will in fact be able to increase our private good consumption.

Indeed, as a matter of simple logic, rational individuals will attempt to balance their goods demands with their leisure demands, so that the utility gain from goods purchased with the after-tax wage from the last hour worked exactly balances the utility value of the forgone leisure to get those goods. We work, in short, to get the things we want.

But this chapter raises the previously ignored question of what if we cannot get, on the margin, what we want by working? Consider in particular the leisure choices that result from desires for pure public goods. Regardless of the extent of a rational individual's desire for a pure public good, each person will recognize that any income generated to acquire it will be inconsequential; the public good outcome is collectively determined, and this is well-known to every individual. Because leisure is scarce and valuable, the typical person who cares about public goods—everybody to varying degrees—will generate too little income.[3] They will equate the marginal value of leisure to the marginal value of private goods but not to the marginal value of public goods, because they cannot individually increment public goods.

Thus, again reemphasizing, using benefit-cost analysis to value pure public goods implicitly starts with a given income that is presumed optimal

when it is, in general, suboptimal.[4] Moreover, all or nearly all of the ungenerated income would have been devoted to the public good (because
there is no incentive to undergenerate income to buy ordinary private
goods). I say nearly all, because as the amount of public goods increase
their marginal values will fall relative to private goods and leisure.

The situation is as depicted in figure 8.1. The level of public good provision is on the horizontal axis, while marginal benefits and marginal provision costs are on the vertical axis. The MB_{True} curve represents the (unob-
served) aggregate marginal willingness to pay for the public good when
there is neither the traditional demand revelation problem of chapter 7 nor
the supply revelation problem emphasized in this chapter. It shows the
marginal willingness to pay if people *could* increment the public good by
their individual decisions to generate income, as they can with ordinary private goods. Leisure and ordinary goods consumption are, in other words,
being *optimally* varied by individuals along MB_{True} at various hypothetical
levels of collectively determined public good provision, G. If larger levels of
G are provided, financed either by taxes or higher private goods prices, one
would expect that households would react by consuming smaller levels of
private goods and leisure, in some mix.

Holding leisure fixed, however, at any level results in steeper conditional
marginal willingness to pay curves. Consider the case of an increment to the

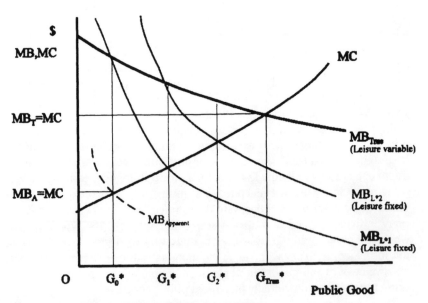

Figure 8.1.   True versus apparent public good optima

public good. The marginal value of forgone ordinary private goods will rise more rapidly if households cannot reduce their leisure to obtain greater income than would be the case if they had that option. Similarly, for decrements to the public good, being constrained to have a larger than optimal income implies that households would be willing to give up more goods to avoid that decrement.

There will be an infinite number of leisure-fixed marginal willingness to pay curves (two being shown in figure 8.1). Each such curve possesses one point at which the fixed leisure constraint is nonbinding. That is, at one level of the public good the fixed leisure will also be the optimal leisure for that public good level—where the fixed leisure curve intersects MB_{True}. In the figure, were there neither demand nor supply revelation problems, the regulatory authority would clearly produce G_{True}^*, the public good level at which true marginal benefits equal marginal provision costs, the one true Samuelson optimum optimorum.

Now, oppositely, assume the presence of the traditional demand revelation problem that rational decision makers are unwilling to reveal their true demands for public goods, because they know they will get—free—whatever happens to be provided anyway and that any revealed demands would negligibly affect the provision level. Additionally, assume that these rational people also will not give up valuable leisure to generate income to buy things that they cannot individually acquire by doing so (the supply revelation problem being emphasized in this chapter). In other words, consider the extreme polar case of the situation that would give rise to the true optimum. Self-interested individuals are generating the wrong income level, and they are unwilling to reveal what public goods are worth to them at that wrong income level. In this extreme situation, the provision level for the public goods will initially be zero, because there will appear to be no demand whatsoever for such goods.

Eventually, the gap between the true marginal benefits and the marginal costs of the public good will result in regulation via the political system (e.g., creation of the Environmental Protection Agency [EPA], passage of an Endangered Species Act, and such).[5] A positive quantity of the public good will be provided, either directly by government or by a regulated private sector, with taxes or prices rising as a consequence. The initial provision level is unlikely to be optimal according to any analytical benchmark.

However, while it is not critical to the argument, assume that the regulators have managed to stumble on a mechanism that accurately reveals aggregate demand out of current income, solving the problem of the preceding chapter. However, the mechanism is not presumed to solve the supply revelation problem of interest in this chapter. The dashed curve labeled $MB_{Apparent}$ in figure 8.1 depicts the marginal benefits observed by the regulatory authorities in this situation, and presumably they would wish to provide G_0^* of the public good, abstracting from any public choice disincentives to do so.

A FALSE AND A TRUE DYNAMIC SCENARIO

If the supply revelation problem of this chapter did not exist, individuals would reoptimize leisure and private goods from their levels at a zero provision level to those appropriate to a G_0^* public good provision level, consuming fewer private goods and buying less leisure (working harder). Hence, the regulators would now, in principle, see a larger demand for the public good, shown as $MB_{L \cdot 1}$ in figure 8.1. $MB_{L \cdot 1}$ is the marginal benefit when leisure is constrained to the level appropriate to a G_0^* provision level, hence it falls faster with G than does the marginal benefit when leisure is variable as previously discussed. Should the regulatory authorities conduct another benefit-cost analysis, they would now find it optimal to provide G_1^* of the public good. At this point, individuals would again reoptimize, resulting in a new marginal benefit curve, $MB_{L \cdot 2}$, which in turn would prompt the regulatory authority to provide more of the public good in the figure, at G_2^*.

This process could be expected to continue if benefit-cost analysis were conducted for reasonably small increments to the public good. If additionally these analyses were conducted with some frequency, one might expect that actual outcomes would come to approximate the true social optimum in figure 8.1. The process described would seem to lead inexorably toward the one true optimum depicted in the figure, with luck approximating it after perhaps only a few benefit-cost iterations.

The preceding discussion of the dynamic process essentially endogenizes the labor supply decision as it relates to public goods provision in a three good world of leisure, private, and public goods.[6] But this description of the dynamic process errs in presuming that individuals will reoptimize their leisure and other goods consumption when G_0^* is provided. Indeed, this is the whole point of the supply revelation problem, individuals will only work to pay the higher costs associated with G_0^*. The regulatory authorities do not observe $MB_{L \cdot 1}$ when the public good is provided at the G_0^*. Rather they continue to only observe the $MB_{Apparent}$ curve.

In going from zero to G_0^*, households decrease leisure (and ordinary goods consumption) somewhat to pay the higher taxes or prices associated with having G_0^*. As with any project offering future benefits (discussed in chapter 3), those public good benefits can only be incremented after first incurring costs (e.g., installing add-on control devices, prior to receiving cleaner air). Any adjustments to income (leisure) and private goods consumption that households would deem optimal as a result of the *costs* of providing higher levels of the public good will also be made *prior* to arriving at G_0^*.

The vertical distance from $MB_{Apparent}$ to the MB_{True} curve represents the (unknown) extent of the supply revelation problem. Were the demand revelation problem relatively more important than the supply revelation problem, $MB_{Apparent}$ would be located further to the right of its hypothetical location in figure 8.1. In such a case, the vertical distance to the MB_{True} curve (the supply revelation problem) would be smaller. Essentially, the regulatory authority only observes a portion of the true demand, assuming optimistically that the demand revelation problem of chapter 7 has been solved.

The labor-leisure endogenization process described in the first two paragraphs of this subsection will, then, be short-circuited. If the regulatory authority were to consider going from $G_0{}^*$ to $G_1{}^*$, the costs would appear to be greater than the benefits, and that movement would be (wrongly) rejected.

The true marginal benefit curve, for normal or superior public goods, such as environmental quality, is itself shifting out over time. Rising real income due to technological advances and innovations (most likely for ordinary private goods for obvious excludability reasons), by increasing the relative abundance of private goods, will cause a shift to the right of both MB_{True} and $MB_{Apparent}$, still presuming the demand revelation problem to be solved.

However, assume for a moment that the relative importance of the demand revelation problem and the supply revelation problem remains constant at higher income levels. A 10% increase in MB_{True} will lead to a 10% increase in each component of that increase, but only the output demand revelation problem is assumed solved. Hence, the rightward shift in $MB_{Apparent}$ will be smaller in absolute terms than the overall shift. In other words, it is not at all clear whether apparently optimal provision levels are getting relatively closer or relatively further from the (moving) true optimum optimorum over time. In the real world, of course, decisions get made and are not revisited with great frequency. So a strong suspicion is that we might be getting further from many public goods optima, *despite* progress in the sense that many public goods levels are increasing. Hence on purely theoretical grounds, public goods are likely to be underprovided employing standard benefit-cost techniques, even with the unrealistic assumption of perfect demand revelation.

MUCH ADO ABOUT NOTHING

What is the practical significance of the supply revelation problem discussed in this chapter? It is certainly the case that the $MB_{Apparent}$ curve in figure 8.1 could have been drawn to represent a larger proportion of MB_{True}.

There is, however, much suggestive evidence that would imply that far too few resources are being devoted to public goods. A first observation is that small alterations in leisure result in income changes that are quite large relative to current spending on most public goods.

Illustrating with the case of environmental quality, our interest here, at the time of his study, Freeman has calculated that the United States spent roughly $225 billion annually on all major environmental programs instituted since 1970, say $240 billion in current dollars.[7] A mere 1% increase in income generated to go toward such environmental goods would amount to $120 billion at a current $12 trillion gross domestic product (GDP). Solving a supply revelation problem of even such small hypothetical magnitude would result in a 50% increase in resources devoted to environmental public goods provision and a substantially improved environmental quality, even with rising marginal provision costs.

Additionally, a robust finding in economics is that decision makers often exhibit a much smaller dollar willingness to pay (WTP) for an item than the minimum amount that they claim to be willing to accept (WTA) to part with it. That is, suppose that you have six cans of green beans in your pantry that cost $1 each. If someone were to ask you how much you would be willing to pay for an additional can, you are likely to say something less than $1 (otherwise you would be likely to have already purchased an additional can). But, if that same person were to ask you how much you would accept to part with one of your cans of green beans, you are likely to say something greater than $1. This is really just the law of demand as discussed in chapter 2—small increases in some good add less to satisfaction than small decreases in the same good subtract from satisfaction, because of diminishing marginal utility.

But in many cases the difference between WTA and WTP seems implausibly large. For ordinary well-known private goods (e.g., coffee mugs or pens), the disparity between WTA and WTP is fairly small (observed ratios of WTA/WTP between one and two). But as the good in question begins to have properties more like a public good, the disparity grows. For example, surveyed individuals might indicate they would not pay much at all for a 1% increase in air quality. When asked, however, how much they would be willing to accept to give up 1% of air quality, they often claim large amounts, often ten or twenty times larger.

There are possibly many explanations for this (endowment effects, moral responsibility, and so on). However, that the WTA/WTP gap is by far the largest for public goods, suggests the possible importance of the arguments presented here. The ungenerated income would add to the WTP, greatly reducing the gap, and suggesting that it is WTA, *as currently measured*, that might more closely approximate properly measured WTP. There is an asymmetry in incentives, with there being (because leisure is valuable) an incentive to free ride for increases in the public good but to increase leisure and private goods in the presence of decreases in the public good.[8]

Additionally, the arguments of this chapter may also account for seemingly faulty environmental perceptions, perceptions that certain conditions are worsening when official data would suggest that they are improving. A large majority of surveyed Americans believe U.S. air quality is deteriorating, while fewer than one out of four believe that air quality has gotten better in recent decades, despite average reductions of 77 million tons per year of EPA criteria pollutants. Clear improvements in environmental measures are being perceived as deterioration. While there may be competing hypotheses (e.g., bias introduced by environmental groups or the liberal media), it is possible that more feels like less, that we are doing better in absolute terms, but worse in relative terms. The growth in real income, and hence consumption of private goods, may well have lowered private good values relative to public good values. It is, of course, relative values that matter in economics.

One might counter the preceding arguments by claiming that Americans work long hours already, hence they are unlikely to be willing to work still harder to obtain higher levels of public goods, such as environmental quality. The discussion of most of this chapter has implicitly assumed, to focus on the symmetric free riding behaviors, that the public good is independent of leisure and private goods. It is clear, however, that Americans do generate a great deal of income to buy private good substitutes for improperly provided public goods. Focusing on the case of location-fixed public goods, one might argue that nonoptimal suburbanization has occurred because of failure to properly provide school quality, low crime, park space, and the like in our urban centers. Provision of such goods need not then necessarily result in a greater net work effort, because costly commuting can be avoided and the desirable urban amenities, say culture or restaurant diversity, can be consumed more cheaply if public goods are properly provided at the urban center.[9]

But the general point of this chapter remains: Only if *perfect* private good substitutes existed for all public goods would households generate the correct amount of income and receive the correct amounts of private and public goods (private and public not being distinguishable in this case). This is highly implausible.

Another counter argument to the importance of the observations being made here is that pure public goods are comparatively rare. Most of the goods we care about are private, hence the welfare loss (recall those areas from chapter 2) from even substantial underprovision of public goods provision might be small. However, the supply revelation problem discussed in this chapter will also emerge for any good for which nonuse value is a significant component of overall value. Consider impure public goods, many of which, while nonexcludable, are rivalrous, the tragedy of the commons case. The use values for such goods may well be fully reflected in resource allocation decisions, as emphasized by Coase.[10] Nonuse values, however, will be understated, not only because of traditional demand revelation difficulties but also because of the supply revelation problem emphasized here.

Particularly noteworthy are contentious issues of preservation (cut the old growth forests versus preserve them, drill for oil or natural gas versus preserve pristine areas, drive a species to extinction versus preserve it, and so on). Such controversies involve clashes among the few with high use values and the many with nonuse values of varying magnitude. Because rational individuals in the latter group will know they are too small to make a difference, they will not give up leisure to generate income for preservation, even in the unlikely case of perfect demand revelation. The resources are more likely to be allocated to their use values, when in some cases that would be nonoptimal.

The implications for the practical relevance of the Coase theorem are clear; both the traditional demand revelation difficulty and the supply revelation difficulty discussed here are likely to result in inefficient resource allocation when nonuse values are important for any good. Indeed, whether a forest is privately or publicly owned, the nonuse values might in some cases swamp in magnitude the use values, leading to resource misallocation when the nonuse values are mismeasured, due to either demand or supply revelation problems. It seems exceedingly unlikely that both problems can be surmounted in practical policy settings.

As mentioned briefly previously, real income (output) has risen dramatically over time in the developed world. This implies that marginal values of ordinary goods will have fallen relative to marginal values of public goods and goods with important nonuse value. The gap between the growing optimal provision of public goods and their actual provision may well be increasing, not decreasing, despite cases of measured progress.

In closing this chapter, the discussion here naturally leads to the policy critical question: "How do we proceed when we do not know how much income would in fact have been generated if households could buy public goods as they can ordinary private goods?" We appear to be in a bind, a bind complicated by the fact that individuals have incentives to hide their true preferences. Though speculative, one possibly fruitful approach would be to increase public goods provision levels until their WTA/WTP ratios approach the much lower levels observed for ordinary private goods. This involves the policy implication that environmental public good projects (e.g., CO_2 abatement) should be done even when they *appear* to have costs greater than benefits.

The problems discussed in this and the preceding chapter are "big-think" problems with the conduct of environmental benefit-cost analysis. For ordinary private goods there are no revelation problems, because there is no incentive to reveal anything but the truth. To attempt to reveal artificially low values merely hurts the dishonest—they either a) do not buy something with true benefits greater than costs or b) do not work when the true benefits of working are greater than the costs.

For public goods, on the other hand, we have a real problem. Such goods will not be produced privately, because their non-excludability renders that unprofitable. Because we cannot directly observe peoples' values in ordinary markets, we are forced to try to guess at what those values are in other ways. Part IV tackles the "small-think" nitty-gritty approaches that are taken in specific settings to attempt to recover true values from individuals who have no incentive to reveal them. We shall see that the various approaches are often flawed and typically in ways that are biased against the environment.

QUESTIONS FOR DISCUSSION

1. Why are individual values aggregated *horizontally* for ordinary private goods and aggregated *vertically* for pure public goods?
2. How likely do you feel it is that people might engage in behavior with personal costs greater than personal benefits for the public good? As the number of people affected by a project gets larger, would you expect such behavior to increase or decrease?
3. Can one really solve the demand revelation problem without solving the supply revelation problem? That is, because both problems reflect failure to accurately reveal demand (out of initial endowments of time and money), might there be some mechanism that handles both problems simultaneously?
4. If regulatory authorities were to increase levels of the public good, would you generally expect households to work more or less? Why?
5. What does WTA mean? How does it differ from WTP? *In general*, which concept would you think would be the most appropriate for the EPA to use when evaluating an environmental policy? Do the arguments of this chapter alter that conclusion? (Hint: what if there is mismeasurement of WTP?)
6. How much variation in true WTP do you think there is across people? If we were more alike in our preferences, might the political system do a better job of providing environmental and other public goods?
7. When households are surveyed about WTP for some environmental improvement, some seem to have implausibly high values relative to their incomes. Might this possibly be due to the fact that it is *current* income that is being elicited, rather than the income that would be

generated if such households actually could buy environmental improvements as they can ordinary goods?

8. This chapter focused on the labor/leisure decision and incentives to overbuy leisure, if you cannot acquire what you want by working. But, will there be similar problems with *any* decisions that involve the generation of extra income? (Hint: one way to get greater income is to acquire more education.)

9. Saving is conducted for greater future consumption (either for one's self in retirement) or for one's descendants. Suppose a household, and all of its descendants, places great value on environmental and other public goods that it cannot individually buy, either now or in the future. Will savings rates be greater or smaller for such a household, relative to those who desire ordinary goods? What impact would this have on the appropriate social rate of discount? Does this situation suggest that perhaps, barring a solution to the free riding problem, different discount rates should be used for public vis-à-vis private goods?

NOTES

1. It should be noted that a) some individuals with pronounced social consciences might work more than would normally be considered rational in this case, b) some individuals will volunteer in an effort to make a difference in that way, and c) some individuals will work in the political arena to acquire what they think socially desirable. In all cases, however, they will do less than is socially desirable, if rational, because personal costs will be large relative to personal benefits of all such actions.

2. P. A. Samuelson, "The Pure Theory of Public Expenditure," *Review of Economics and Statistics* 36 (1954).

3. In the heterogeneous preferences case, it is likely that even a quantity of the public good that is socially suboptimal will be too much for some individuals, perhaps the poor and healthy in the context of the environment. For those individuals, the income undergeneration argument of the text evaporates; the supply revelation problem in this case becomes a nonbinding disincentive.

4. It would be implausible to suggest that decision makers might accidentally hit on the one true Samuelson optimum optimorum, resulting in optimal work-leisure decisions. To do so would require, even with perfect demand revelation out of current income, that decision makers accept public good projects with costs in excess of benefits (out of existing income) by the amount of the ungenerated income that would have been devoted to public goods were individuals able to purchase them as ordinary private goods. As with the demand revelation problem, individuals have no incentive to accurately reveal that information to decision makers.

5. The gap discussed in the text will be growing over time with a positive ordinary income elasticity of demand for the public good, creating ever-increasing political pressure to intervene.

6. See for greater detail, N. E. Flores and P. E. Graves, Optimal Public Goods Provision: Endogenizing the Labor/Leisure Choice, manuscript, 2002.

7. A. M. Freeman, "Environmental Policy since Earth Day I: What Have We Gained?" *The Journal of Economic Perspectives* 16 (2002): 125–46.

8. This sentence presumes independence between the public good and either private goods or leisure; there could, of course, be either a complementary or substitute relationship that would modify the text assertion.

9. See http://spot.colorado.edu/%7Egravesp/WPSuburbanization2-22-02.htm for greater detail on the oversuburbanization that stems from the failure to properly provide central city public goods.

10. Ronald, J. Coase, "The Problem of Social Cost," *Journal of Law and Economics* 3 (October 1960): 1.

IV

PRACTICAL PROBLEMS WITH THE IMPLEMENTATION OF BENEFIT-COST ANALYSIS

In part I it was argued that the voluntary supply and demand interactions of the market system (and its analog for public goods) will lead to perfect decisions, if we possess perfect information about tastes, technology, and prices. This would be true for decisions at a point in time and for decisions regarding projects with benefits and costs occurring over lengthy time periods. Part II emphasized that the rosy scenario of part I only occurs when there are no missing markets. Externalities and public goods were discussed as two important cases where failure to charge prices that accurately reflect scarcity leads to the wrong relative amounts of environmental and other goods—to relatively too few environmental goods and too many ordinary goods. The Coase theorem was seen as a reason why environmental problems are not more prevalent, but the conditions under which it is valid are restrictive. Part III examined the flawed incentives that people have to accurately reveal their preferences for public goods, further diminishing the practical significance of the Coase theorem for both the economist and the environmentalist.

In part IV we now turn to the study of how economists and others go about actually determining the position and shape of the marginal benefit and marginal cost curves in a world of *imperfect information*. Chapter 9 presents information on how the costs of environmental control policies are estimated. That there is but one chapter on costs and several on benefits reflects the greater uncertainty on the benefits side, hence the many approaches toward their estimation that require discussion. Chapter 10 provides an overview of the benefit estimation chapters, giving a sense of the types of approaches, before going into the more in-depth critiques that make up chapters 11 through 15.

The various methods of benefit estimation embed a wide variety of underlying assumptions, assumptions that often are not only dubious but that are also in many cases inconsistent. One approach, for example, requires that people be *perfectly* aware of the variation in pollution and the damages associated with pollution—as knowledgeable about these goods as they are of the nature of a can of tomato soup or a cup of steamed broccoli. Another approach assumes, oppositely, that those damaged by pollution have *zero* perception of what is causing their damages and how those damages would vary over space, for otherwise people would employ various (costly) mitigation strategies.

Each approach yields marginal damage estimates (and marginal damages *are* the marginal benefits of cleanup). But how are we to think about those estimates? Are they alternative estimates? Because the assumptions about perceptions of damage differ so dramatically this would seem unlikely—they are almost certainly picking up different damages, some perceived and some not. Yet, to add the damages together might be likely to lead to double counting of some damages. In all cases, however, what we are seeking is an accurate measure of *marginal willingness to pay* for environmental benefits that can only come at the cost of forgone other goods that we also care about.

9

Approaches to Estimating the Costs of Environmental Control Policies

As emphasized in chapters 1 and 2, costs have little to do with dollars per se. Rather, the fact of scarcity—that we cannot have everything we want with the resources available to us—forces us to make choices. In the environmental setting, this means that we face a trade-off between environmental goods and other goods that we would also like to have. Choosing more environmental quality inevitably (apart from so-called no regrets policies that are rare[1]) means that we must have less of other goods—the forgone benefits from those goods are the costs of the decision to have more environmental quality.

However, analysis of the cost side of environmental decision making is often made easier by the fact that many environmental control costs do handily come in the form of dollars, which makes it easier to add them up and to compare them to benefits (assuming we meaningfully put the policy benefits in dollar terms)[2].

TYPES OF ENVIRONMENTAL POLICY COSTS

There are essentially three types of control policies. The most commonly used policy in the United States and many other countries is that of *required add-on controls*. The catalytic converters required on all automobiles built after 1974 is but one example of this approach. The second type of cost is *required input or output substitutions*, with the substitution of low sulfur Western coal for high sulfur Eastern coal or other pesticides for DDT being examples. Both of these approaches tend in practice to be applied uniformly (e.g., *all* new cars being required to have catalytic converters,

109

whether registered in Los Angeles, California, or Laramie, Wyoming; or banning of *all* uses of DDT). The final approach, that of *spatial or temporal relocations*, takes advantage of the fact that marginal damages (hence the benefits of a policy) vary greatly over space or by time of year. An example would be required siting of power plants downwind from major population centers rather than upwind. We shall consider each of the three approaches in turn, before turning to the role of economic incentives in environmental policy.

Examples of required add-on control devices are everywhere. Catalytic converters for vehicles have already been mentioned. But, wet and dry sulfur dioxide scrubbers are often required for power plant smokestacks and for some other industrial point sources.[3] Also in common use are so-called baghouses, which operate much like the bag on a home vacuum to eliminate particulate matter from flue gases, though of course much larger.

Calculating the present value of the expected costs of an environmental control policy under this approach involves merely adding up the discounted values of all the resources employed as a result of the policy. Any add-on control device will involve the use of some mix of capital, labor, natural resources, and energy. Many of the costs, for example capital, will not be discounted much because they occur up front, while many other costs might require considerable discounting, as for example the labor or energy necessary to keep the control device running smoothly over its projected life.

Required input or output substitutions, and other process changes, are also quite common. This approach involves substituting a more expensive but less polluting input or output for its less expensive and more polluting counterpart. An important example would be requiring the use of Western coal, which has approximately one-third of the sulfur content of Eastern coal.[4] The substitutions may be complete as, for example, the bans on DDT, chlorofluorocarbons (CFCs), or certain types of asbestos. Or the approach might be partial, with some important uses of the damaging input or output being allowed while others are not.

Illustrating, suppose that a firm has chosen an input combination that is lowest cost (to maximize profits) for the output level it is producing. The input combination chosen might not, of course, be the lowest cost from society's perspective, allowing for external costs. For example, a long-lived chlorinated hydrocarbon pesticide, such as DDT, might be chosen by a farmer as least cost. But, there might be many external damages (bio-amplification of pollution concentration moving up the food chain, damages to aquifers, runoff damage, and such) that cause the social cost of this approach to be quite high. Substituting from DDT to, say, malathion (which has a far shorter residence time in the environment, breaking down into harmless subcomponents) might be far less costly when all costs are considered. Not only might the substitute product be more expensive because it is less effective, but the farmer might also need several applications rather than just one. Hence the private costs might be substantially higher, despite the lower social costs, if external damages are large.

In such cases, a required substitution might make a great deal of sense. Usually, however, outright bans are seldom optimal, for reasons that will be clear from the supply-and-demand discussion of chapter 2. Some uses of the substance under consideration for the ban might be of great importance (e.g., banning saccharin to a diabetic, who is unable to tolerate sugar), while other uses are less important. The all-or-nothing approach of banning is a blunt instrument in many such cases. A properly set tax on such goods might discourage frivolous uses while at the same time allowing high value uses to continue.

As with add-on control devices, the cost of required input or output substitutions is usually fairly easy to determine, at least relative to benefits. The cost of the substitute will be higher either because more must be used, because a given quantity has a higher price, or both. To an Eastern power plant, for example, Western coal costs more because of shipping, while more of it also has to be used because it has a somewhat lower British thermal unit (BTU) rating than Eastern coal.

Finally, although either implicitly or explicitly not even *allowed* in most current policy, spatial or temporal relocation of pollutants sometimes offers a low cost alternative way of reducing total damages from residuals in the environment. This approach does not reduce total emissions but moves them—at a cost—to where they do less environmental damage. A given amount of emissions into the atmosphere can have different impacts depending on how those emissions affect air quality (which varies) and how many damage receptors there are to experience the reduction in air quality (which also varies).

Illustrations would probably be useful. Some locations, such as the South Coast Air Basin that contains Los Angeles, California, are frequently subject to stagnant air conditions, resulting in high concentrations of ambient air pollution. Other locations, such as Chicago, Illinois, have generally dependable replacement of dirty air with clean air from prevailing, relatively steady, winds from the West. So, any given amount of emissions can have different impacts on air quality; and it is air quality that affects utility, not emissions per se.

Similarly, holding constant the relationship between emissions and air quality, the relationship between air quality and damages (benefits of control) depends on how many people and things people care about are present to be damaged. To emphasize perhaps the most important case, population density is on the order of 1,000 times greater in large urban areas than in rural areas (perhaps 6,000 people per square mile versus 6 people per square mile in a rural location). This means that, all other things being equal, any change in air quality would cause 1,000 times more damage in urban areas than in rural areas.

Of course, all other things are not always equal—we might care greatly about locations with few people (e.g., the Everglades or Grand Canyon), desiring to keep such places pristine. But nonetheless it is clear that for one to say, "I don't want to just move pollution around, I want to eliminate it!" is in general irrational, ignoring many policies that can have benefits far greater than costs. Those proposing new power plants, by way of illustration, have been required for many years to present alternate possible locations with an eye to incorporating trade-offs between private costs and social costs in the final decision of where such plants are located. Perhaps belaboring this, merely locating a power plant downwind rather than upwind of a population center might greatly reduce local damages, while the transmission distance to customers might be similar in either location. Such site review policies could be usefully expanded, because damages from any given amount of pollution can be orders of magnitude smaller or larger depending on where they occur.

Water pollutants, called effluent rather than emissions, can similarly be located so as to minimize damages to water quality. It matters whether an oxygen sag (lowered oxygen content in water with changes in the nature of viable flora and fauna) occurs where commercial and recreational fishing is important or not. Similarly, water quality will be more important at a beach or municipal water inlet than at other locations.

The timing of emissions, whether air or water emissions, can also matter greatly. Air emissions during an inversion (where relatively cool air is trapped against the ground by higher level warm air) can result in extreme accumulations of pollution in the atmosphere. Environmental policy might well impose stricter standards, even to the point of shutting down polluters and restricting transportation mobility at such times. Similarly, effluent into high temperature and low flow streams (as at certain times in the late summer in many locations) can do far more damage than emissions into those same rivers and streams at other times (e.g., during spring runoff with high volume, cool waters that contain more oxygen, and better dilution of any pollutants present). Many such policies can have benefits greater than costs.

The spatial or temporal approaches do not, however, address global environmental problems; problems, such as global warming, will be unaffected by such local or regional policies. Still, once the global concerns are addressed with optimal controls, it will remain the case that relocations over space or time can yield additional benefits for mankind and the environments that we value.

THE ECONOMIC INCENTIVE APPROACH

Why have we taken the approaches to environmental policy that we have? Why, in particular, have we modeled our control policies largely on the old Soviet system of command and control? Just as the Soviet planners told industrial firms what and how to produce, EPA policy makers in the United States tell emitters how they must produce to get a given environmental outcome (e.g., required catalytic converters to obtain a given auto-related air quality). Yet the rest of the economic system is not that way at all, either in the United States or in most of the rest of the democratic world.

The reason we have what is, almost certainly at this time, an archaic method of getting improved environmental quality is related to the fact that we were a rich country before we had much in the way of environmental monitoring capacity. That is, for both required emission controls (e.g., catalytic converters, scrubbers, and baghouses) and for process change controls (e.g., Western coal for Eastern coal), it was *much* easier to observe whether the controls were met, than to observe whether they had any impact on air quality. This was because actually monitoring air quality, in the way necessary for an effective economic incentive approach, was not possible.

Suppose, for example, that bureaucrats just said to car companies in the late 1960s when controls were first implemented, "We don't care how you do it, but we want your cars to be ten times cleaner beginning in five years than they are now." This did not happen because monitoring how much pollution was coming out of the tailpipe of an automobile was at that time expensive; indeed, it was completely impractical to suggest that we might be able to know how much pollution is coming out of every single car (new and old) on the road, as modern tailpipe inspections currently allow at reasonable cost. Similarly to charge a major sulfur emitter per ton of sulfur dioxide (SO_2) requires that we know how many tons they emit. This requires continuous monitoring, because polluters might choose to emit at night or other times when they cannot be easily observed by regulators, this being particularly so for water polluters.

So in the early days of pollution control, it was much easier to see whether a smokestack scrubber or catalytic converter was in place than it was to have any sense of whether the air was actually getting cleaner and at reasonable cost. Indeed, neither the power plant nor the household automobile driver cared whether the pollution control device actually worked; they only cared whether they had it, meeting the letter of the law requiring it.

There are two major problems with the approach of required add-on controls and required process changes. First, requiring firms and households to take particular actions might not be the least costly way to obtain the same outcome—either might know of less expensive ways to achieve the same result. For example, requiring a SO_2 scrubber might be *much* more expensive for certain power plants than substituting low sulfur Western coal that might achieve the same level of air quality. Second, neither the firm nor the household has any incentive to care whether the device required *actually works*.[5] Once they have met the letter of the law they have no strong economic interest in whether we get the environmental quality that was hoped for when the legislation requiring the device or process change was imposed.

In recent years, continuous monitoring has become quite low cost, and emission inventories are available for most pollutants for most major locations. The ability to monitor pollutant emissions is critical to being able to harness the forces of the market to clean up our air and water. The other critical condition for the economic incentive approach to work well is that there must be variation in costs of cleanup among polluters. If a ton of SO_2 pollution costs the same to eliminate regardless of industry, age of plant, and so on, there can be no substantial benefits from the economic incentive approach. How do economic incentive approaches work?

Economic incentive approaches work by encouraging those who are best at fighting pollution to do so. There are three basic types of economic incentive approaches to reducing pollution. Salable emission rights will receive the most attention here, because it is in somewhat more common use and is the likely approach to ultimately be taken in limiting worldwide CO_2 emissions.

What is to be established by the following simple example is that any given level of environmental quality can be achieved at least social cost (scarce labor, capital, and other resources) if those who are most efficient at fighting pollution receive incentives to do so. Suppose our objective is to reduce SO_2 pollutant discharges into the air from one million tons to 700,000 tons per year. Ideally, the decision of how much to lower pollution would be based on a balancing of marginal benefits and marginal costs, but this is not at all critical to the advantages of the economic incentive approach. Even if the required cut in emissions is completely arbitrarily chosen, we would still want to achieve the goal at least cost.

Consider a simple production system with five different types of firms described in table 9.1. The first column lists the five firm types, labeled A through E. The second column indicates how much is emitted from each type of plant, with plant type A, for example, emitting 300,000 tons of SO_2 per year. The third column provides information about the cleanup costs of each firm type which have been ordered from highest to lowest.[6] The numbers are actually fairly realistic, because salable emissions rights, while highly variable, have frequently been in the $200 to 300 per ton range.[7]

Table 9.1. A Demonstration of the Efficiency of the Market Incentive Approach

Firm	SO_2 Emitted (thousands of tons)	Cleanup (cost/ton, $)	COST (Policy 1)	COST (Policy 2)	COST (Policy 3)
A	300	$500	$150x$500=$75M	$90x$500=$45M	-$0-
B	200	$400	50x$400=$20M	60x$400=$24M	-$0-
C	200	$300	50x$300=$15M	60x$300=$18M	-$0-
D	200	$200	50x$200=$10M	60x$200=$12M	200x$200=$40M
E	100	$100	-$0-	30x$100=$3M	100x$100=$10M
TOT	1,000,000		=$120,000,000	=$102,000,000	=$50,000,000

The next three columns represent the costs of cleaning up 300,000 tons of SO_2 under various policies.[8] Under policy 1, no firm is allowed to emit more than 150,000 tons of SO_2. Firm A would have to eliminate one half, 150,000 tons, of its pollution, at a cost of $75,000,000. Firms B, C, and D would each have to eliminate 50,000 tons of pollution under this policy at a cost of $20,000,000, $15,000,000, and $10,000,000, respectively. Firm C is unaffected by this policy, despite being best at fighting pollution, because its current emissions are below the allowed 150,000. The costs of this policy add up to $120,000,000, but it achieves the goal of eliminating 300,000 tons of SO_2.

Policy 2 is a rollback policy in which each firm is required to decrease its pollution by 30%. This policy, too, would eliminate 300,000 of the million tons of one million current tons of SO_2 emissions. Under this approach, Firm A must eliminate 90,000 tons of pollution (30% of 300,000 tons), which would cost it $45,000,000. Similarly, Firms B, C, and D must eliminate 60,000 tons each, with Firm E required to begin cleaning up as well. The total cost of eliminating 300,000 tons of SO_2 under this policy would be $102,000,000 (lower than under policy 1 because the lower cost of cleanup firms just happen to be doing more of it).

Policy 3 is the salable emission rights policy. Under this policy, each firm is assumed to be granted the right to emit up to 70% of last year's pollution.[9] What will happen? Firms having a high cost of eliminating SO_2 will want to buy the rights to emit if they can buy those rights for less than the cost of cleanup. Similarly, low cost of cleanup emitters of SO_2 will want to sell the rights to emit if they can receive more than their cost of cleanup for those pollution rights. The case is as depicted in figure 9.1.

Because Firm A would be willing to pay as much as $500 to emit, the demand for the first 300,000 rights to emit is $500. Firm B would only be willing to pay up to $400 to continue emitting the 200,000 tons it emits, and so on. In the absence of a limit on emissions rights, the firms would collectively emit 1,000,000 tons of pollution.

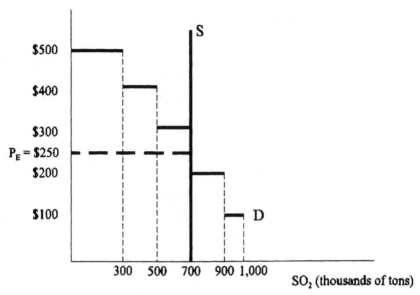

Figure 9.1.   The demand and supply of SO₂ emission rights

However, the supply of rights to emit is now only 70% of last year's pollution, which will result in high cost of cleanup firms (such as Firm A) wanting to buy the rights to pollute from low cost of cleanup firms (such as Firm E). Because of the somewhat peculiar step function form of the demand curve in this case,[10] the equilibrium price is not specific but will end up somewhere between $200 per ton and $300 per ton; assume for simplicity that it is $250 per ton.

It is easy to see the incentives that are created by this emissions rights market. Firm A will want to buy the rights to emit 90,000 tons of pollution, because it has the right to emit 210,000 (70% of last year's emissions). This will cost the firm $$22.5 million dollars, but note that a -$0- is entered in the cost column for policy 3 in table 9.1. This is because the dollars are mere transfers; Firm A is not changing its production in any way, hence has the same real cost as before. It is using neither more nor less of society's scarce resources. We will look at the financial transfers a bit more at the close of this example, but for now recognize that only Firms D and E will be changing their behavior.

It is in the interests of Firms B and C to also buy rights to pollute rather than clean up, because their cleanup costs are $400 per ton and $300 per ton, respectively, and they can buy the right to pollute for $250 per ton, less than their cleanup costs. Each of these firms will purchase 60,000 tons of emission rights (because they already have the rights to emit 140,000 tons,

70% of last year's pollution), paying $60,000 ($250 per ton) or $15,000,000 each.

Total payments for the right to pollute then are the $22.5 million from Firm A, plus the $30 million from Firms B and C. These dollar amounts are received by Firms D and E, who are the sellers of emission rights. Firm D is better off by $50 per ton of pollution for every ton it cleans up, because this firm can clean up for $200 per ton while selling the rights to a ton of emissions for $250. So Firm D will sell all 140,000 rights to pollute that it was assigned. Similarly, Firm E will sell its entire allotment of 70,000 rights to emit, because this firm can clean up for $100 and sell the rights to pollute for $250.

A total of 210,000 rights to pollute are exchanged at the $250-per-ton price, with the dollar costs to buyers being transferred to sellers, hence washing out from society's perspective. But, note that the salable emissions rights approach, policy 3, results in *less than half the cost* in terms of society's real scarce resources when compared to the traditional command approaches of policies 1 and 2. These results, while stemming from a purely hypothetical example, are in fact quite real world, with the market incentive approach typically costing 20% to 50% of traditional approaches. This is because Firms D and E, the firms that are relatively good at fighting pollution, are encouraged to do so under the market incentive approach.

There are many additional benefits associated with the economic incentive approaches. First, because environmental quality is less expensive with these approaches, ordinary downward sloping demand curves would suggest that we would want to buy greater amounts of environmental improvement at its lower price. Additionally, environmental groups could advertise intentions to buy rights to pollute, without exercising them.[11]

Another major advantage of the economic incentive approach is that it encourages economic growth *without* environmental degradation. Suppose the demand for the output of the firms in table 9.1 goes up and they wish to produce more output, which would normally result in greater emissions of SO_2. Because they have no more rights to pollute than before the increase in demand, they must enter the emissions rights markets with greater demands. This might drive the price of emissions up to $350 per ton or so, at which point Firm C would begin cleaning up and selling its rights to pollute.

Similarly, suppose a new polluting firm opens up in the area of the five firms in table 9.1. This firm, because it has no history of emissions, receives no initial emissions rights, hence must buy those from existing firms. This will again increase the price of emission rights, encouraging all existing firms to engage in greater cleanup efforts. Thus even with economic growth the level of pollution does not go up; indeed, at higher per capita income levels, it is likely that we would desire a smaller supply of emissions rights.

What about alternative approaches involving economic incentives? Consideration of figure 9.1 should make clear that if authorities were to charge a pollution tax of $250 per ton, exactly the same outcome would occur. Firms A, B, and C would merely pay the tax, while Firms D and E would clean up rather than pay the tax. Note, however, that having to pay a tax is analogous to having to buy *all* of the rights to pollute, rather than being allocated some initially. This would make the polluting firms less profitable and would result in smaller polluting industries over time than is the case with firms receiving free rights in a portion of last year's pollution.[12]

One of the reasons many economists and environmentalists prefer salable emissions rights to pollution taxes is that under the salable emissions rights approach, the environmental outcome is *certain*, and what is uncertain is the sales price of the allowed emissions rights. Under the tax approach, it is the tax that is certain, while the environmental outcome is uncertain.

Reiterating the goal of this chapter, we are seeking information on costs of environmental policies that are accurately measured to compare to our best guesses at the environmental benefits associated with those policies. Clearly, costs have been higher historically than necessary because of the historical approaches of command and control, rather than reliance on the economic incentive approaches that have had such success in the market system as a whole. The economic incentive approaches result in pollution being cleaned up by those who are best at cleaning up, in much the same way that any other market good is produced, in equilibrium, by those who are best at producing it.

Hence, a major source of upward bias in estimation of the costs of environmental policies is associated with failure to use economic incentive approaches that would be expected to lower costs. Another source of upward bias stems from technology forcing, which occurs when an environmental policy (say, salable emission rights) sets in motion entrepreneurs who will seek lower cost technologies for eliminating pollution to sell to polluters who wish to avoid having to pay for the rights to pollute. Additionally, there is learning by doing, in that the more one repeats an activity the better one gets at it (e.g., falling prices of catalytic converters as familiarity with their production and use increases). Moreover, there are the usual sorts of mass production economies that are often not fully considered when an environmental policy is first being discussed. Overall, it is likely that costs of an environmental policy are overstated.[13]

QUESTIONS FOR DISCUSSION

1. Most of the examples of this chapter related to production by firms. Can you think of some examples of required add-on devices, input or

output substitutions, or spatial/temporal changes that apply to the household sector? (Hint: these are more common than you might think, both in the home and on the road.)

2. Can you think of how the costs of various environmental policies that you know about fit into the taxonomy introduced at the beginning of this chapter?

3. In the text, a ban on some polluting activity or good was referred to as a blunt instrument. Thinking in terms of the supply and demand diagrams of chapter 2, why was this assertion made?

4. Can you think of some examples of policies that might have benefits greater than costs that shift the location or timing of pollution emissions of various sorts?

5. Why were the purchases of the emission rights not considered to be costs in the discussion of salable emission rights?

6. Imagine a sixth firm, like one of the other five firms in table 9.1, comes into existence. What happens to figure 9.1? The equilibrium price of emission rights? The level of pollution?

7. It is sometimes argued that costs of various projects are *understated* rather than overstated (a rough rule of thumb one hears is that actual costs will be twice what the costs were estimated a priori to be). Why is this less likely to be the case for environmental projects?

8. Why does a tax of $250 per ton emitted result in the *same amount* of short-run pollution as does a subsidy of $250 per ton for each ton not emitted?

9. Rank taxes, subsidies, and salable emission rights according to which would lead to the smallest size of the polluting sector in the long run.

NOTES

1. A policy is referred to as a no regrets policy if it provides benefits with zero or *negative* costs. For example, many people are unaware that replacing ordinary incandescent light bulbs with low wattage fluorescent bulbs would be *both* cheaper and provide environmental improvements (less energy generated with reduced pollution and CO_2 buildup). Another example might be an aluminum recycling effort that ends up being profitable.

2. Some people believe that it is not only difficult to put health and other environmental benefits in dollar terms but that it is also morally wrong to do so. But whether morally wrong or not, such a process is inevitable; the health effects are going to occur or not occur whether we think about them or not. To make rational decisions requires that we compare the advantages with the disadvantages of a decision, so some weighting must occur. To do that unavoidable weighting in dollar terms is just a matter of convenience.

3. For both air and water, sources of emissions (for air) or of effluent (for water) are broken into point sources, where the pollution exits via a smokestack or pipe,

and non-point sources where the origin of the pollution is less concentrated. For water, examples of non-point sources would be urban parking lot runoff of oil/detritus or agricultural runoff of fertilizer or pesticides into local streams, rivers, or oceans. For air, the non-point sources are household emissions from furnaces, fireplaces, and the like along with large emissions from the transportation sector, usually subcategorized into mobile sources.

4. In a political world, such required substitutions, while often efficient, might not happen because of losses of jobs and tax revenue in regions disfavored by such regulations. If, on the other hand, the economic incentive approach is used, such substitutions become voluntary individual firm decisions and not subject to political maneuvering. The role of politics and jurisdictions will be taken up in detail later in the text.

5. Indeed, many households (an estimated 8% to 13%) substituted the then-available, and much cheaper, leaded gasoline for unleaded gas in cars with the newly required catalytic converters. It turns out that just a few tankfuls of leaded gas coated the catalytic converters, rendering the car roughly 100 times dirtier.

6. It should perhaps be emphasized that there is no necessary relationship between the volume of pollution produced by a plant and how costly it is for the plant to clean up. Large polluters, like Firm A, could have low costs of cleanup and small polluters, like Firm E, could have high costs of cleanup. Similarly, one would not expect that the costs of cleanup would be the same *within* any given plant for each ton cleaned up—rather one would expect that each plant might have some pollution that could be eliminated cheaply and other pollution that could only be eliminated at high cost. The numbers in table 9.1 are purely hypothetical.

7. The Chicago Board of Trade (CBOT) has been auctioning SO_2 permits since 1993. For much more detail on the specific workings of this program, see www.chicagoclimatex.com/education_ccfe/SO2_Background_Drivers_Pricing_PDF. pdf.

8. The policies are representative of actual policies, but many other types of policies exist, for example, that require a specific add-on control device. It should be clear from the text discussion cost savings resulting from the economic incentive approach would hold for a wide variety of specific policies—after all, a required device could always be *voluntarily* purchased if that turned out to be optimal for a particular firm.

9. It is not the least bit critical to the analysis that the firms be given 70% or even *any* rights to pollute. Each firm might be required to purchase rights to any amount of pollution from the EPA or from you for that matter. Who gets to sell the rights to the (reduced) amount of emissions is a matter of equity, but as a practical matter the rights are usually distributed to existing emitters in proportion to prior pollution.

10. The odd shape stems from the simplifying assumption that each firm has a constant cost of cleanup for each ton emitted. This is unlikely to be the case in practice, because each of the firms will have some pollution that can be cleaned up more cheaply than other pollution. This would smooth the demand curve. Moreover, the more firms there are in the market, the greater the number of steps in figure 9.1—for a large number of firms the demand curve would also take on the normal downward sloping appearance of the demand curves in chapter 2.

11. This approach would not eliminate the free rider problem, but it might well be more effective than appeals that involve competing with deep-pocket polluters in efforts to pass pro-environment legislation.

12. It should be noted that a subsidy can achieve the identical *short-run* outcome as a tax (or salable emissions rights). Paying firms $250 per ton to eliminate pollution, rather than taxing them, creates the same incentive to eliminate pollution; firms D and E would accept the subsidy and eliminate pollution. But subsidies make the polluting industries more profitable rather than less profitable vis-à-vis taxes and salable emissions rights. Hence subsidies result in a non-optimally large polluting sector in the long run.

13. It is certainly the case that costs are often understated for many projects (e.g., airports, dams) undertaken by government. The politics of such cases is rather different, though, with powerful interests wanting to get paid to create the project. If anything, such forces would be reversed for environmental projects, that often have powerful political enemies.

10

Overview of Approaches to the Valuation of Benefits of Environmental Policies

The preceding chapter considered how one goes about estimating costs of an environmental policy. It was argued that costs of environmental policies, while easier to estimate than benefits, are nonetheless likely to be overstated relative to the actual costs that will be incurred. In this chapter, an overview of various approaches to the estimation of environmental benefits is given. It is argued here that the various approaches are likely to result in undervaluation of benefits.

As a first important observation, damages are not *directly* related to the reductions in emissions that stem from an environmental policy. It is not emissions, per se, that give rise to damages but rather changes in environmental quality that result from reductions in the emissions. Environmental quality is certainly related to emissions, but the relationship is far less direct than is usually supposed. There are two reasons for this. First, depending on air or water characteristics, a reduction in emissions or effluent might have a large or a small impact on environmental quality. If air is stagnant or stream flow is low and warm, a given reduction in emissions might have important impacts on improving environmental quality.

Second, given the impact on environmental quality, the extent of damage reduction (hence the benefit of cleanup) will depend on how many damage receptors receive the improved air or water quality stemming from the policy under consideration. Recall from the first principles of chapter 1 that it is *human* preferences that matter from the economists' perspective, and if what humans care for is not harmed by pollution—regardless of any environmental effects due to the pollution—benefits of cleaning up pollution will be nonexistent.[1]

There are four principal approaches to the estimation of environmental benefits. Each categorical approach has advocates and critics. Recalling the previous discussions of the underlying motives for our willingness to pay for environmental improvements (use value, option-to-use value, bequest value, and preservation value), it will be seen that some methods will do a better job at getting at certain motives and a rather poor job at inferring other motives. We will briefly introduce the four approaches in this chapter, with chapters 11 to 14 providing greater detail.

REFERENDA

In democratic societies voting is a popular approach to determining whether an environmental project has benefits greater than costs. The many "green" propositions in California provide examples of this method. The idea is to describe, in as much detail as is practical, the benefits and costs of a policy and allow a majority of the citizenry to vote the policy up or down.

The principal drawback to voting is that it fails to reflect the *intensity* of individual wants, which is particularly important when either the benefits or costs are unevenly distributed. That is, if a person has a compromised cardiopulmonary system and will die unless a policy is voted in, all he or she can do is vote for that policy. If the majority of healthy voters have even slight excesses of costs over benefits, a policy with overall benefits far in excess of costs might be voted down.

Note that the problem of intensity of wants does not exist for ordinary market goods—if people have really strong desires for, say, clothing, they will spend a higher percentage of their income on it. However, one advantage of voting is that it might at least partly overcome the free riding problem. You know that you are not going to have to pay for the good unless the policy passes; hence you know that everyone else will also be paying. Because voter turnout is typically quite low in the United States and in many other countries, it is also problematic in that the preferences of many individuals may not be included.[2] And, there are some peculiar voting paradoxes to be discussed in greater detail later.

SURVEYS, INTERVIEWS, AND EXPERIMENTS

One approach to determining individual values for environmental projects is being used with increasing frequency and this approach is to merely ask, in one way or another, individuals whether a project is worthwhile. This can be done with detailed surveys and interviews or in experiments involving, in many cases, real money. The main difficulty with this approach lies with interpreting the results. Are people revealing true willingness to pay or are they merely expressing environmental attitudes? There are a great many additional specific problems with this approach (strategic bias, starting point bias, selectivity bias, wording bias, hypothetical bias, vehicle bias, sequencing bias, and so on), and it is highly controversial.

One reason for the growing popularity of this approach, despite heated controversy, is that it can explicitly get at nonuse values. Use values tend to be much better estimated than the various nonuse values (e.g., preservation values), but even small individual nonuse values can add up to large amounts if enough people possess those values. In some situations, we have no choice but to attempt to obtain information in so-called constructed markets, because there is no other way to obtain that information.[3]

SUM OF SPECIFIC DAMAGES

The sum-of-specific-damages (SSD) approach to valuing environmental improvements is intuitively plausible, but it is not without difficulty in both implementation and interpretation. As emphasized at many points in this book, the benefits of pollution cleanup are the damage reductions resulting from a policy. The SSD approach to estimating the benefits of cleanup merely adds up physical damage reductions and puts a dollar value on them. While there are, of course, many different types of damages associated with pollution—morbidity, mortality, materials damage, crop damage, and aesthetic damage—this approach typically is only undertaken for health effects, and is sometimes referred to as the health effects method. The process is as follows:

1. For each damage category, determine how much reduction in physical damage will occur as a result of the policy (e.g., a reduction of 1 microgram (μg) of SO_x, say going from 17 to 16 μg, may save twenty-three lives in the New York metropolitan area).
2. Multiply the damage reduction by a valuation, the valuation being (ideally) the marginal willingness to pay for the reduced damages (e.g., personal valuations of changes in the probability of death in many settings have been estimated at between $5 and $7 million dollars—say, $5 million. Thus, the lives saved would be worth 23 x $5 = $115 million).
3. Do the preceding—at least in principle—for every physical damage that the policy would reduce (e.g., more bushels of soybeans times their market price, various morbidity measures times their values, improved length of time between painting homes times that value, and so on).

4. Add the dollar values up—this will give you the marginal benefits in convenient dollar terms to be compared with the dollar costs of the policy.

The main problem with this approach is that there is great scientific uncertainty about both the physical effects and the values to be placed on them. How many asthma attacks will not take place if ozone is reduced 10% by a policy? What is it worth to have one fewer asthma attack, $20 or $100? These are difficult questions. Moreover, this approach implicitly assumes that the health (and other) effects just happen to people and that they are unaware of how such effects relate to pollution. If people *were* aware how the damages they experience related to pollution, they would be expected to mitigate those damages by changing their behavior in various ways (e.g., by installing pollution filters, by moving, by not exercising on high pollution days, and so on). Such changed behavior, while costly, is not picked up in the SSD approach.

USING KNOWN RELATIONSHIPS BETWEEN
ORDINARY GOODS AND ENVIRONMENTAL GOODS

In a sense, the preceding SSD approach could have been included here—a damaged person perhaps visits a hospital when the pollution levels go up, as they might under other circumstances. The expected benefit of visiting the hospital has to be as least as large as the cost of a visit, so that cost represents a lower boundary to the benefit associated with damage reduction.

But a rather different, more indirect approach is envisioned under this category. The three primary subapproaches to this approach are a) property value hedonic valuations, b) wage hedonic valuations, and c) travel cost valuations.

The notion underlying property value studies is that the value of homes (sales prices or rents) will be related to the traits that the homes possess. Consider the typical real estate multiple listing information. A listing will contain information about the structural traits of the home (construction of stone or wood, number of bathrooms and bedrooms, age, type of heat, square footage, family room, garage, special features, and so on) and about the traits of the neighborhood in which the home is located (schools, access to the city, ocean, or mountains, and so on). Those traits will, collectively, determine the value of the home. But one of the traits that people care about is environmental quality—a home in a polluted area will rent or sell for a smaller amount than will a home in a cleaner area, all other things being equal. If we can determine how much people are willing to pay for an equivalent home in a clean location versus a dirty location, we will have a measure of exactly what we want, the marginal dollar willingness to pay for environmental quality, which can then be compared to the dollar marginal cost of environmental quality. The property value benefit estimates stem, then, from a statistical relationship between property values and all of the variables (including pollution) that determine those values.

A quite similar technique attempts to value variations in environmental quality by looking at labor markets rather than land markets. The idea is that some labor market regions are more polluted than others and that people will have to be compensated for the pollution they experience to be willing to work in dirtier cities. That is, if City A (one of two otherwise identical cities) has higher pollution levels than City B, residents would move from A to B, reducing the labor supply in A (raising wages) while increasing the labor supply in B (lowering wages). The movements would continue to occur until the wage differential just compensated people for the higher pollution in City A. Again, if this approach seems plausible, it has the desirable feature of getting exactly what we want, the marginal willingness to pay in dollar terms, which can then be compared to the marginal costs of policies yielding that amount of cleanness. As with the property value approach, wages are statistically related to pollution, holding constant other wage determinants (e.g., education, experience, occupation, region, and so on).

Travel cost methods of valuing environmental goods depend on the following presumption: The value of the things we visit must be at least as great as the full cost of getting there. Imagine, for example, a world composed of zones around some natural wonder (e.g., the Grand Canyon). Those nearer would be expected to have higher visitation rates than those farther away, because they have lower costs of visiting the site. One can calculate the cost of visiting the site for people in any zone, using explicit out-of-pocket costs as well as implicit time costs, any entrance fees, and so on. Those costs can then be related to visitation rates, with lower rates being observed at higher costs. In this way, a demand curve can be generated. The value of the natural wonder, then, is the area under the estimated demand curve.

There are a number of problems, to be discussed in detail in chapters 14 and 15, associated with each of these approaches. The biggest single problem with the hedonic approaches is that they implicitly make *exactly the opposite* assumption made with the SSD approach about perceptions of how damages relate to environmental quality. For the SSD approach to work well, how damages vary with environmental quality must be unperceived, or otherwise people would attempt to minimize those damages, incurring costs of doing so. But for the hedonic methods to work well, people have to have *perfect* information, not only about where it is clean and where it is dirty, but also what such variations mean in terms of health and other impacts on individual households.

The perceptions issue raises a crucial question: If SSD picks up unperceived damages (e.g., complicated health effects about which little are known) and the hedonic methods pick up perceived damages (e.g., smells or views), should the damages be added together? In practice, they are not. There would almost certainly be some double counting if they were to be added together, but at the same time the damages that are perceived and the damages that are not perceived might be mostly different types of damage. This would indicate that it would be appropriate to aggregate the estimates of damage from the two approaches.

Moreover, as we shall see in chapter 14, it turns out that the estimates of damage from property value studies should be *added to* the estimates of damage from wage studies. It would be irrational to pick a labor market entirely based on wage rates, without looking at property values and available amenities. A dirty city will have *both* higher wages and lower property values in general than a clean city, hence the separate effects should be added together. Again, in practice they are not.

In this chapter, we have taken a look at the general approaches to valuing environmental amenities, without going into great detail about the strengths and weaknesses of the individual methods. Over the next few chapters, we will examine the approaches in much greater detail. During this process, a common thread will emerge, namely, that the approaches used to value environmental goods tend to undervalue those goods.

QUESTIONS FOR DISCUSSION

1. How much error is likely to be introduced into benefits estimation by failure to properly model the dispersion of environmental pollutants into air or water? Can simply assuming that air quality will be improved in proportion to pollution removed result in accurate measures? Will this depend on the nature of the pollutant?

2. Which of the various approaches to obtaining estimates of environmental benefits do you think would work best for the various motives underlying willingness to pay for environmental benefits? That is, people value the environment for use, option to use, bequests, and for preservation, which methods will work best for each of those motivations?

3. Which of the various approaches discussed in this chapter do you favor? Why? Do your answers to these questions depend on the nature of the environmental policy under consideration?

4. What housing variables would need to be held constant in a property value analysis? For a wage compensation analysis? What would happen to the estimates of the effects of pollution if some important vari-

ables were omitted from the equations? Would your answer depend on whether those variables are correlated with the pollution measures that are included?

NOTES

1. This is not really quite as restrictive as it might at first blush seem. Most of mankind's pollution is emitted in close proximity to large population centers where large-scale production occurs. One might make a case, at least for local or regional pollutants, that if we properly take care of *our* species, other species (generally at greater distance from the pollution) are not likely to be greatly harmed. This argument breaks down, as we shall later discuss, for transnational and global pollution problems.

2. It could be argued that it is appropriate to ignore the preferences of those not voting, because they may be presumed to not have strong preferences or they would have voted.

3. A major controversy with this approach involves whether *any* number is really better than *no* number at all. This approach will result in numbers—stated values for willingness to pay—but as indicated briefly in the text the validity of those numbers is hotly debated.

11

Voting as a Way to Confer Environmental Benefits

Voting has a lot of appeal in democratic societies. While this is understandable, it is also the case that voting has some undesirable properties in many contexts. If all policies had the property that either benefits were greater than costs or costs were greater than benefits for *every* voter, there would be no problem—policies would be passed or rejected unanimously, and properly so. But, benefits and costs are typically unequally distributed among voters; in particular, suppose that a small minority have strong preferences for an environmental improvement (benefits far exceed costs), while a majority have a small excess of costs over benefits. In such situations, a policy having overall benefits substantially in excess of costs, an efficient policy from society's collective perspective, might be voted down by a large majority of voters.

Illustrating, suppose that a small community of 5,000 households is contemplating an environmental cleanup policy costing $1 million ($200 per household) that is expected to prevent two people from dying, with no other benefits. As is actually realistic, nobody knows who the two people will be, but perhaps 10% of the people—those with weakened cardiopulmonary systems—think they have a chance of being one of the unlucky two. For the 90% of households who strongly suspect they will not be affected, rational self-interest would lead them to vote against the policy, having costs ($200) exceeding their negligible benefits. For the 500 households who think they might be affected, all they can do is vote for the policy. The discrete for or against choice eliminates consideration of the intensity with which one is for or against, hence it is a blunt instrument for getting at properly measured aggregated net policy benefits.

While there is considerable debate about what the value of a statistical life (VSL) should be, nobody who has seriously studied the issue believes that the so-called VSL is less than $500,000,[1] as would be required for the lopsided vote that will emerge in our example to be efficient. At this writing, the EPA is currently employing a $6 to $7 million VSL. Using such numbers in our example would suggest that a policy that has benefits greater than $12 million, and costs of only $1 million might be voted down by a 4,500 to 500 margin; nine to one against a policy with benefits exceeding costs by an order of magnitude!

The problem of course is that voting fails to reflect the intensity of wants of the individual voter. This is not a problem for ordinary private goods, because if individuals *really* desire a good, they can always buy more. Others, with low intensity of wants for a particular good, do not have to buy it at all. For collectively provided goods, however, we all get the level that is governmentally determined, which will be too much for some and too little for others.[2] It is quite common for costs of environmental policies—despite being much lower than benefits in many cases—to be spread broadly over society (say, higher electricity bills or increased taxes). This presents an efficiency problem for the provision of such goods, though on equity grounds many continue to favor voting outcomes.[3]

It should perhaps be emphasized at this point that special interests (which we will return to in chapter 15)—small groups with either high benefits or high costs from a policy—are nonetheless still legitimate interests. Benefits are benefits and costs are costs regardless of how concentrated they are, but if they are concentrated in a few individuals those individuals will clearly want to try to get or avoid them, respectively. Whether it is a person not dying who receives a large benefit from an environmental policy or a person paying the high costs of society's desire to preserve old growth forest, these special interests are still interests that should be incorporated in the benefit-cost analysis. As discussed in more detail later, it is only when those having concentrated benefits or costs are able to distort the accuracy of benefit-cost analyses that the concentration, per se, becomes a problem for pursuit of efficient policies.

Another potential problem with voting is the paradox of intransitive preferences where the power to set the agenda determines the actual outcome. Illustrating, suppose we have three individuals (there could be many more people of each type) and three potential policies. Aaron, Bob, and Cathy have the following rankings for policies 1, 2, and 3, where > means preferred. Aaron prefers policy 1 to policy 2 and prefers policy 2 to policy 3, with Bob and Cathy having different rankings as shown.

Putting some concrete environmental policy implications for this seemingly abstract case, consider the case where policy 1 is a stringent environmental control policy for diesel engines, policy 2 is somewhat less stringent,

Table 11.1.   The Voter Paradox: Intransitive Preferences

	Policy 1	*Policy 2*	*Policy 3*
Aaron	1>	2>	3
Bob	2>	3>	1
Cathy	3>	1>	2

and policy 3 is a nonstringent no-control policy base case. For present purposes, it does not matter which policy is either more efficient or more equitable; but suppose policy 1 is the most efficient (diesel fumes are quite damaging to health), and policy 3 is viewed as most equitable (diesel truck and car drivers are viewed sympathetically).

If we were to do a pair-wise comparison of policies 1 and 2, which would be preferred by majority voting? Clearly, Aaron prefers 1 to 2, as does Cathy; hence, policy 1 will be selected over policy 2 with a two-thirds majority. The more stringent policy is preferred over the somewhat less stringent policy. And for the comparison between policy 2 and policy 3, policy 2 is seen to be preferred to policy 3 by a two-thirds majority consisting of Aaron and Bob. The less stringent policy is preferred to the nonstringent no-control case. Thus, policy 1 is preferred to policy 2, and policy 2 is preferred to policy 3. So one would certainly suspect that policy 1 should be seen as best, right? Well, let us now compare policy 1 with policy 3 in exactly the same pair-wise comparison. Aaron likes policy 1 better than policy 3, but both Bob and Cathy prefer policy 3 to policy 1. Social preferences over policies can be intransitive in this way (transitivity is a property of the real number system, e.g., 10 > 8 and 8 > 6 implies that 10 > 6, but also of rational individual preferences[4]).

We have a potentially important real world political problem here: Whoever controls the agenda setting process can control the outcome in settings like this. That is, suppose that those determining which policies, among several being considered, get voted on have received PAC contributions from diesel engine and automotive producers. In committee, if the slate setters decide to go forward with the efficient policy 3 and the equitable policy 1, the representatives of the various constituencies will select policy 3, because two-thirds (Bob and Cathy) prefer it. The agenda setter, in short, can exert far more control on the outcome than we would really like in a voting democracy under some circumstances.[5]

A related, but more general problem is that the inability to make interpersonal utility comparisons means that we can never know with any degree of confidence that any policy will make society better off.[6] Even if the policy rankings happen to be unambiguous and benefits are greater than costs, expressed in dollars, it is the case that we do not know what those dollars *mean* to the people receiving or paying them. For example, a policy that gave benefits to Bill Gates or Donald Trump that were twice the magnitude of costs to ordinary citizens, while efficient, might be viewed as undesirably inequitable. Indeed, policies of pure transfers from the rich to the poor are neutral with respect to efficiency (the benefits equal the dollar costs, assuming no loss in the transfer processes), but people feel strongly about such policies on equity grounds.[7]

One desirable feature of the market for ordinary goods is that (in the absence of market imperfections of the type discussed in chapters 4 and 5) exchanges are "Pareto efficient," after Vilfredo Pareto, an Italian economist. A policy is said to be Pareto efficient when it makes one or more individuals better off, while making nobody worse off. Because nobody is harmed, and some (conceivably all) are helped, society as a whole would seem to clearly be better off if such policies are pursued. Moreover, few reasonable people would object to Pareto efficient policies on equity grounds except in extreme cases.[8]

However, unlike voluntary exchange of ordinary private goods, one must strongly suspect that all social policies having B > C for *everyone* (or for some, while harming nobody, in particular non-benefiting taxpayers) are likely to have already been done. Hence, we cannot *know* that a policy makes society better off, even when its benefits exceed its costs.

Recognizing this practical problem with the notion of Pareto efficiency leads to the concept of "Kaldor-Hicks efficiency," after Nicholas Kaldor and John Hicks, two English economists. A project or policy is Kaldor-Hicks efficient if those who are made better off *could* compensate those who are made worse off, whether the actual compensation takes place or not. It is the Kaldor-Hicks efficiency notion that underlies the benefit-cost analysis discussion of chapters 2 and 3. If no group is systematically discriminated against, and if we enact large numbers of policies, always doing things with benefits greater than or equal to costs in dollars (despite the non-comparability of their meaning among individuals) society as a whole is made better off *on average*. While any particular policy might hurt a group of concern (e.g., inspection-maintenance policies for the control of automobile pollution, which predominantly harm the poorer drivers of older cars), it is expected to be offset by some other policy (e.g., food stamps, housing vouchers, or a more progressive tax system). So while it is the case that all Pareto efficient policies are Kaldor-Hicks efficient, most of the latter are not efficient under the more stringent standards of Pareto efficiency. It is also the case that a Kaldor-Hicks efficient policy can be converted to a Pareto efficient policy, if the winners do *in fact* compensate the losers (because *if* overall benefits exceed costs, a fraction less than one of the dollar benefits can be transferred to the losers to make them indifferent or better off). With the vast number of often small policies being implemented annually in any large economy, even performing the analysis of who is helped and harmed would be impractical, would, that is, itself be a policy with $B < C$.

The point, really, of this discussion is that one has to make policy (the policy of doing nothing is still a policy). Pareto efficient policies are exceedingly rare, but Kaldor-Hicks efficient policies offer the ray of hope that efficient policies need not be inequitable, as long as no groups are systematically discriminated against in the policy setting process.

A couple of other observations about voting: First, the well-known rational voter ignorance problem might render outcomes dubious for complex environmental referenda. The costs of knowing much about an environmental policy to be voted on might be fairly high, but the benefits will usually be vanishingly small. What are the odds, after all, that any individual voter will be decisive in the vote, even in situations in which they care a good deal about the outcome? This suggest that busy voters might not really think much about the policy they are voting on, if they vote at all.[9]

One additional voting problem leads to an unknown efficiency bias. It is only the marginal voter that matters to politicians running for office or advocating for or against an environmental referendum. That is, if Republicans always vote for the Republican politician or the Republican policy recommendation and if Democrats always vote for the Democratic politician or Democratic policy recommendation, those voters will be ignored by candidates or those writing the environmental referendum. It is only the swing voters that matter in such cases. If, for concreteness, the Sierra Club says that they can deliver fifty thousand votes, in a close Senate election, for the candidate who agrees to vote for an environmental bill working its way through Congress, that might well have an impact on whether a politician of either stripe agrees to support the bill. The lesson, for environmentalists, is to become organized, joining environmental groups that can be perceived as delivering the all-important marginal voters.

The overall policy implication of this chapter is that voting, while a popular mechanism in democratic societies, is unlikely to be a good way of conferring net benefits of a policy. Many environmental policies have relatively concentrated benefits (going disproportionately to the sick or rich, for example) along with dispersed costs from a typical voter's perspective (going to everyone, and probably disproportionately to the middle class and poor in many cases). Thus it is likely that voting biases outcomes against the environment, with resulting environmental quality being inefficiently low. This is particularly the case if those who are most immediately affected by the costs are able to affect the agenda setting process, as discussed in the context of the voting intransitivity paradox. Other issues might provide partial offsets to this bias (e.g., not voting by those affected little by the issue), but failure to reflect intensity of want results generally in lower than efficient environmental quality levels.

QUESTIONS FOR DISCUSSION

1. In what situations would you expect voting to lead to an undesirably low level of environmental quality? An undesirably high level? Which situations are most likely to occur in practice?
2. Why is it imperative that we attempt to determine the VSL? As the probability of death gets bigger, what would you expect to happen to the VSL? Is it fair or appropriate for the VSL in Africa or Southeast Asia to be one-twentieth of that for the United States or another developed country? What are the efficiency and equity issues? Should the VSL be adjusted for age? What are the efficiency and equity issues?
3. In light of the discussion of Pareto versus Kaldor-Hicks notions of efficiency, how do you feel about whether the owner of an old growth forest should be compensated for preservation? Would how you feel change if you knew the owner to be rich?
4. How likely do you feel it is that environmental policies would be subject to the voting paradox (that aggregate preferences might be intransitive, with behind-the-scenes agenda setters wielding great power to determine outcomes)?
5. It was argued here that it is impossible to know what a "dollar's-worth" of benefits or costs *means* to any individual. Would you generally expect a dollar to be worth more to a rich person or to a poor person? Does this mean we must always pay great attention to who is helped or hurt by any particular policy?
6. Which do you think is of greater importance in introducing bias into decisions made via voting, rational voter ignorance or the importance of the marginal voter? Do these potential sources of bias in the outcome always work against environmental policies? For them?

NOTES

1. As with any value, what we are seeking is marginal willingness to pay. For the case of VSL, it is a change in the probability of death that we wish to value. On the one hand, the probability of a specific individual dying from some environmental pollutant is likely to be low; but, in a rich country safety has a high value. From studies relating wages to risks of death on the job, studies relating seat belt use, and related approaches, recent (1997) VSLs in the range of $0.7 to $16.3 million dollars are being observed with a mean of $6 to $7 million in current dollars. This number would be expected to get larger with rising income and with higher probability

events. For the most recent numbers, and more detail on VSL, see the website of the EPA.

2. Interestingly, we are likely to be fairly near the social optimum when arguments between those who want more and those who want less are most vociferous. If the benefits of improved environmental quality were either far below or far above costs, the amount of disagreement would be smaller. Again, this differs from the situation for private goods, because everyone can have—individually—exactly what they want at the market equilibrium.

3. There are also cases in which costs of an environmental policy might be concentrated while benefits are widely dispersed. For example, suppose a landowner is contemplating cutting down a large stand of old growth forest, with an anticipated profit of $15 million dollars. Those concerned about the loss of the habitat might attempt to get a law passed to prevent the logging. This might or might not, on efficiency grounds, be an efficient policy, depending on whether the preservation values exceed $15 million. But on equity grounds, is it fair that one household should have to pay for the preservation benefits received by all?

4. Would it not seem extremely odd if you were to overhear someone saying "I like ice cream better than mashed potatoes, and I like mashed potatoes better than broccoli . . . but I like broccoli better than ice cream." Such preferences are non-Darwinian in the sense that, with goods of different market value at stake, repeated voluntary trades could extract all of the wealth of those with intransitive preferences.

5. While one might suspect that such cases are rare, one must realize that "all the easy stuff" has already been done (everything that we all agree on—we should have a national defense, a set of laws, a fair court system has already been done, leaving things about which there is more disagreement).

6. This observation came to be known as the Arrow Impossibility theorem, after Kenneth Arrow demonstrated that no voting system can possibly meet a certain set of reasonable criteria (too detailed to delve into here) when there are three or more options to choose from. The theorem came from Arrow's Ph.D. thesis with the condensed version titled "A Difficulty in the Concept of Social Welfare," *The Journal of Political Economy* 58, no. 4 (August 1950): 328–46. This was later expanded to Arrow's 1951 book *Social Choice and Individual Values*, 2nd ed., (1951; reprint New Haven: Cowles Foundation, 1963).

7. One tends to believe that we are each more similar than different, and if we had identical preferences, a strong argument could be made that income transfers from the rich to the poor make society better off. The rich, under these circumstances, lose less satisfaction from a marginal dollar than the poor gain. The logical problem with this argument is that the rich *might* have gotten that way because of an abnormally high desire for goods relative to leisure—in this case, taking a (high-value) dollar from the rich and giving it to the poor could actually make society *worse* off. The problem is that we cannot see into the heads of different people and know what an additional dollar means to them.

8. If envy is sufficiently important to people, the text statement is not always true. There is evidence, for example, that many students prefer a situation where they receive four lollipops and everyone else receives zero lollipops to a situation in which they receive ten lollipops and everyone else receives fifteen lollipops. If *relative* wealth position in a society matters more to people than *absolute* wealth position, then even Pareto efficient projects will not be universally pursued.

9. This is one possible offset to the bias introduced by voting's failure to reflect intensity of want. It is certainly the case that those with intense wants *will* at least vote. If those without concentrated benefits or costs do not vote, the end result could more closely approximate efficiency. This fortuitous outcome is unlikely, I think, because of the swamping effect of the large number of people who vote for reasons unrelated to personal costs and benefits (e.g., civic pride or the feeling that one must vote to legitimize later griping).

12

Constructed Markets: Stated Preferences and Experiments to Infer Environmental Benefits

In this chapter we consider approaches to valuing environmental goods that involve the construction of artificial markets. There are two general subapproaches: a) stated preference approaches and b) experimental approaches. Stated preference approaches involve direct elicitation of environmental values in hypothetical markets, essentially asking people to reveal their willingness to pay. Such approaches are controversial but have been used to address real world problems in a wide variety of settings, from valuing health care and food safety to the more specifically environmental concerns of this text (e.g., both surface and ground water quality, wilderness and wildlife preservation or reintroduction, and improvements to air quality, particularly visibility). Although there is controversy about whether the numbers one gets from stated preferences approaches are reasonable approximations of true willingness to pay, it must be emphasized that this is essentially the *only* way to measure nonuse (often called passive use) values.

The second approach typically involves experiments using student subjects linked together via computers in which subjects reveal their preferences, with real (albeit typically small amounts) dollars at stake. This approach has often been used to test fundamental assumptions of economic theory (e.g., in game theoretic situations, do the players get revenge even when that is irrational? Or how rapidly does free riding behavior increase as group size is increased?). But experiments are increasingly being used for valuing specific environmental goods and institutional arrangements (e.g., attempts to infer how much emission rights in CO_2 emissions might fall in price from a hypothetical increase in their number).

Most of the emphasis here will be on stated preferences, because this approach has received far more emphasis in the literature on environmental economics, with many thousands of papers published and others on their way to being published. The most widely known application of stated preferences was to the legal damages to be assessed for the 1988 *Exxon Valdez* oil spill in Alaska, but the courts have upheld the use of contingent valuation in other settings as well (e.g., for "Superfund" hazardous waste dumps).

Whether concerned about endangered species, air quality, or water quality all stated preference applications begin with some sort of survey instrument. The survey instrument attempts to create a hypothetical market that will, ideally, be treated by the respondent as if it were a real market.[1] This is a daunting task, because the instrument must both describe the environmental good in a meaningful way to allow benefits to be assessed and it must explain how much payment will be needed to acquire the described good through the so-called payment vehicle.

In the traditional so-called contingent valuation approach, survey respondents are typically asked about the amount they are willing and able to pay for the commodity being valued. It is emphasized to the respondents that receipt of the environmental good is contingent on enough aggregate respondent willingness to pay for the good. Another type of stated preference approach is referred to by the cryptic name conjoint analysis and refers to situations in which respondents are asked to rank, rate, or choose among commodity packages that typically contain several attributes, including price as one among many traits. Still other studies are of a favor/not favor binary choice type. The nature of the good to be provided is carefully explained, along with how much it will cost. By randomly varying the cost given to respondents, researchers can obtain the distribution of the willingness to pay for the good. Much like a dose response relationship in biology, the percentage of people willing to pay different amounts can be determined. From the distributions obtained, mean and median willingness to pay can be inferred.

How accurately do the numbers obtained in these various ways relate to true willingness to pay? It is difficult to answer this question, for many reasons. In some cases it is precisely the distinction between use and nonuse (e.g., preservation) that is of interest, yet it is difficult to untangle the separate motivations that underlie willingness to pay. Another common worry, particularly for "badly conducted" studies, is whether the respondent is merely revealing environmental attitudes rather than the desired willingness to pay.

A laundry list of potential problems would include:

1. Strategic bias? (Do respondents provide many zeros or large numbers in attempts to move the average value closer to their true value?)
2. Hypothetical bias? (Do respondents take the survey seriously?)

3. Selectivity bias? (Are respondents representative of the general population? Those less interested are less likely to complete surveys.)
4. Starting point bias? (Do respondents give different willingness to pay numbers if one starts high and comes down or starts low and comes up? A payment card approach with randomly located numbers to be circled by the respondent largely eliminates this problem.)
5. Sequencing bias? (Do respondents give different willingness to pay numbers depending on whether an environmental good is at the beginning of a sequence of potential projects or at the end? Do many projects, when separately surveyed with different respondents, add up meaningfully in terms of total value consistency?)
6. Interviewer bias? (Is the willingness to pay of the respondents influenced by the demeanor of the interviewer?)
7. Question wording bias? (Is the willingness to pay of the respondents influenced by how questions are worded?)
8. Protest zeros? (Do respondents with true positive willingness to pay amounts express a zero as a protest regarding whether they *should* have to pay or not?)
9. Outliers? (Should respondents with a stated willingness to pay be thrown out when their values seem implausibly large?)
10. Mean or median willingness to pay? (One might reasonably argue that mean values are what is most appropriate for use in benefit-cost analysis, but median values will correspond more closely to voting behavior, hence are of interest to politicians.)
11. Willing to accept or willingness to pay? (For most projects that involve increments in a public good, the willingness to pay is appropriate, but is it measured correctly? As discussed in chapter 8, willing to accept [WTA] is much larger than willingness to pay [WTP], but respondents are asked about their *current* income, not the income they *might* generate if the policy is adopted.)

As is clear from the (incomplete) list here, there are many problems with the practical implementation of contingent valuation. Part of the controversy about this method is that while some specific studies seem well-conducted and convincing, others do not. Is this method an art or is it a science? Can the results be replicated?

Concerns such as the preceding about the reliability of contingent valuation led the National Oceanic and Atmospheric Administration (NOAA) to form a panel of eminent experts—chaired by two economists who won the Nobel Prize—to examine this valuation method. After lengthy public hearings and review of many written submissions, this panel concluded "CV studies can produce estimates reliable enough to be the starting point for a judicial or administrative determination of natural resource damages—including lost passive-use value."[2]

There is some evidence that contingent valuation results in valuations that are similar in magnitude and highly correlated with those coming from other methods, when both methods can be applied (e.g., hedonic analysis or travel cost methods discussed in chapter 14). This is comforting, but the more important observation is that for nonuse values there is typically simply no alternative method for eliciting willingness to pay values. Many environmental policy decisions are costly; much is at stake. Some economists are distrustful of both survey methods and of nonuse values that they elicit. However, a well-conducted survey showing large nonuse values provides information of great value to policy makers, information that is necessary to allow balanced decisions regarding use or nonuse of environmental resources.

QUESTIONS FOR DISCUSSION

1. How likely do you think it is that people will accurately reveal willingness to pay by merely being asked to do so?
2. Would you expect the better quality contingent valuation studies to be more or less costly than lower quality contingent valuation studies? Why?
3. How important do you think nonuse values are relative to use values? Does this vary with the nature of the environmental good under consideration?
4. Can a constructed market ever have the potential to replace a missing market? Or is there something inherently different about markets with required dollar payment versus hypothetical dollar payment?

NOTES

1. See, for an extensive recent analysis of stated preference techniques, I. Bateman, et al., *Economic valuation with stated preference techniques: A manual* (United Kingdom: Department for Transport, UK and Edward Elgar Publishing, 2002). For an accessible introduction see R. Carson, "Contingent Valuation: A User's Guide," *Environmental Science & Technology* 34, no. 6 (2002): 1413–18.

2. See K. Arrow, et al., *Federal Register* 58 (1993): 4601.

13

The Sum-of-Specific-
Damages Approach

The sum-of-specific-damages (SSD) approach to valuing environmental improvements recognizes explicitly that the benefits of cleanup are equivalent to reductions in damages. This approach is sometimes referred to as a health effects approach, because the damages usually considered are related to morbidity and mortality. Although this approach is remarkably simple and intuitive, we shall see that it is fraught with two types of uncertainty and is, moreover, likely to provide downward biased damage estimates.

The idea under the SSD approach is to first gauge how much an environmental policy will reduce physical damages, ΔD, of a wide variety.[1] Then, values, V, are placed on each category of damage, with for example a prevented life lost being valued a great deal and the prevention of an asthma attack much less. The marginal benefits—to be compared to the marginal costs—of the policy will, then, be the sum of all of the reductions in physical effects times their respective values:

13.1 $\qquad$ Marginal benefits $= \Sigma(\Delta D)\$V$

Illustrating, suppose that if a policy is enacted it will save six lives and eliminate one hundred cases of chronic bronchitis. If a saved life is worth $6 million dollars and an eliminated case of chronic bronchitis is worth $300,000, then the policy would have benefits of 6 x $6,000,000 + 100 x $300,000 = $66,000,000. If these are the only benefits of the policy, and it can be put in force for $66 million or less, it would be efficient to adopt the policy because it would have marginal benefits greater than or equal to marginal costs.

The preceding example can be used to illustrate all three major problems with the SSD approach. First, the physical effects due to the policy, ΔD, are highly uncertain; although we supposed that six people would not die and one hundred would not acquire chronic bronchitis if the policy is put into effect, such estimates are uncertain. In testimony prior to the implementation of the environmental policy, some experts may argue that the damages prevented will be large, while others will argue that the damages prevented may be small. In part this stems from advocacy positions—an expert working for the American Lung Association is more likely to predict more bronchitis cases prevented by the policy than an expert working for the National Association of Manufacturers. The final determination of damages will likely depend on some mix of the credibility or credentials of the experts and the quality of the analyses they present.

Where do experts of either stripe get their information? Three primary approaches are clinical studies, epidemiological studies, and toxicological studies. Clinical studies are used to address research questions that can be well examined in laboratory settings. In a human clinical study, scientists investigate the effects of individual air or water pollutant "doses" by measuring a variety of health effects (e.g., lung function, heart rate variability, blood component analysis). Using analogous approaches in vitro (or in vivo in animal surrogates for humans), the way pollutants generate their molecular effects can be discovered. Animal and in vitro studies are particularly important when human data are unavailable or when such data cannot be ethically obtained.

Epidemiological studies, while less rigidly controlled, offer more natural settings through the statistical analysis of data from human populations or by field studies. In some cases, researchers follow fairly large groups of individuals and use detailed questionnaires to relate the incidence of various disease endpoints to pollutant levels. Field studies involve fewer individuals and employ repeated assessments of health effects of pollution exposure. The smaller numbers of subjects involved in field studies allow researchers to extend the information obtained in large-scale epidemiological studies by including measurements of clinical health endpoints. Various epidemiology studies have, for example, implicated particulate matter in premature death among elderly individuals with cardiopulmonary disease and to increased use of medications, doctor visits, and hospital visits for individuals with pulmonary disease, such as asthma.

Toxicology studies attempt to identify and study the specific properties and constituents of various pollutants that are responsible for causing adverse health effects. Toxicologists test the molecular, cellular, and systemic effects of pollutants in experimental settings using cell and tissue cultures, animals, and computer models. Findings of dose response effects from a toxicology study might, in turn, prompt the initiation of a clinical trial or an epidemiological investigation.

Knowledge is gained from the various approaches, but there remains great uncertainty at the policy level about how physical effects relate to pollution exposures. This is particularly so for *chronic* pollution effects, such as perhaps a long latency cancer, vis-à-vis the more immediate *acute* effects.[2] When certain physical effects are difficult, for various reasons, to tie to pollution, they will tend to be ignored in the SSD approach, leading to understatement of damages. Death or cancer have clear definitions, but certain forms of pain, dermatitis, neurological effects, various endocrine disruptions, and the like are difficult even to quantify, let alone relate to pollution, hence are likely to be ignored in practice.

Returning to the example of how equation 13.1 might be used, the second source of uncertainty is what values to place on the physical effects that are predicted to occur. Is the VSL $6 million? Or, is it one-tenth or ten times that? Could the value of a chronic bronchitis case be an order of magnitude greater or smaller than the $300,000 illustration?[3] One might argue that values such as these are at least plausible, and one could make a fairly strong case for the argument that there is greater uncertainty regarding the physical effects than there is regarding the values to place on them.

Neither of the uncertainties discussed to this point would seem to point to any obvious downward bias in damage estimates. There are two important reasons to suspect that such a downward bias exists, however. First, the physical effects should be *all* of the physical effects that will occur as a result of the policy, not just (a portion of) health effects. If a policy cleans up the air or water, it will have physical benefits of a wide variety, not just mortality and morbidity. There will generally be ecosystem improvements, agricultural crop yield benefits, material damage reductions (e.g., house painting with less frequency), benefits for pets, as well as aesthetic effects (e.g., smells, visibility). Because we get all of those effects as a result of the policy they all should be counted, yet they never are.[4]

The situation is as depicted in figure 13.1.

In the figure, health benefits are depicted as comprising a portion of total benefits, and if decisions are based only on health effects, $E_{Too\ Little}$ will be produced relative to the optimum at E^*. The welfare loss from an environmental quality that is too low is depicted by the shaded area in the graph.

There is another theoretical and practical problem with the SSD approach that suggests that too little environmental quality will be produced. For this method to work well as a measure of pollution damages, people have to be unaware that pollution has any impact on the damages. That is, the impact of pollution on, say, health has to either be unknown to us or we have to be unable to determine where it is clean and dirty. The environmental source of the damages has to be *unperceived*.

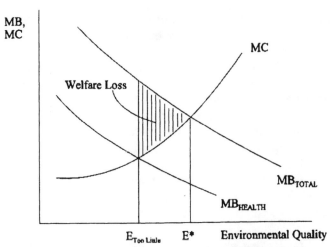

Figure 13.1.   Welfare loss from failure to include all marginal benefits in SSD

Clarifying, it is implicitly presumed that the physical effects just happen to us (we get sick or die), but we do not know why; in particular, we cannot suspect that air or water pollution is damaging us or we would engage in (costly) behavioral changes to avoid those damages. We might not, for example, exercise outside on high pollution days, we might install dust filters or air conditioning in part to avoid air pollution, we might move to a less preferred but cleaner location, and so on. In the case of water, we might buy distilled water or install water filters as a means of avoiding damages from polluted surface reservoirs or aquifers. In all of these cases, we are expending our scarce resources *to avoid* a damage that otherwise would have happened. To merely count the damage that continues to occur, ignoring such costly mitigating expenditures, understates true damages . . . hence understates the benefits of cleanup.

In the following chapter we will examine a method that requires *exactly the opposite* assumption to be accurate. The hedonic method assumes *perfect perceptions* of both environmental quality at various locations and the *entire* impact of environmental quality on our well-being.

QUESTIONS FOR DISCUSSION

1. To be able to determine what change in damages, ΔD, will occur as a result of an environmental policy, we must model the dispersion of air and water pollution. Why?

2. Which do you feel is more uncertain about an environmental policy being contemplated, the change in damages or the values to be placed on those changes?

3. Does uncertainty per se cause a bias in the marginal benefit estimates? If, as seems likely, pure uncertainty is undesirable (e.g., most people would prefer to have $1,000 with certainty than a 50/50 chance at either $0 or $2,000) how would you incorporate this fact into benefit-cost analysis? Might you want to attempt to determine the cash monetary equivalent of the uncertain outcomes in the numerator of the analysis?

4. What were the two arguments that this chapter made regarding why the SSD would be expected to lead to estimates of environmental damages that were downward biased, hence estimates of the benefits of cleanup that were downward biased? Which of the two do you think is the most important as a source of bias?

NOTES

1. Atmospheric modelers for the case of air or hydrologists for the case of water would first be required to model how much environmental quality is predicted to change in various locations as a result in the changed pattern of residuals resulting from the environmental policy under consideration. That is, there would have to be *some* impact on residuals (possibly just moving them to a location where they do less damage) for there to be any impact on environmental quality, and what that impact will have on environmental quality at various locations will need to be modeled. The damages reduced will then depend on how many damage receptors are present in locations with improved environmental quality.

2. Acute effects are easier to study, clinically or epidemiologically because study participants can be tracked with reasonable accuracy over short time periods. Diseases that take many years of exposure to emerge are more difficult to study, because study participants move to different locations. This is a particular problem in that those with the weakest immune systems are the most likely to move to less polluted places, but they are likely to also die or exhibit other endpoint effects at higher rates wherever they locate. Hence the health impact of dirty air is understated when the more unhealthy individuals move to cleaner places.

3. Frank Ackerman and Lisa Heinzerling place particular emphasis, in their well-written *Priceless: On Knowing the Price of Everything and the Value of Nothing* (New York: New Press, 2004), on the notion that the prices used in benefit-cost analysis are so meaningless that the approach is fatally flawed and that refinements of the type discussed in this book are unlikely to make a meaningful difference to that conclusion. I feel that benefit-cost analysis, at a minimum, aids in the ranking of the vast number of potential policies that could be pursued. It offers the potential to identify really bad or really good policies. For a detailed review of the Ackerman and Heinzerling book, see http://spot.colorado.edu/%7Egravesp/BookReviewPrice

less.pdf. The review is also available in *The Journal of Economic Literature* (March 2005): 188–90.

4. One of the reasons many whole categories of damages are ignored in benefit-cost analysis is that we have (irrationally) broken our environmental quality standards into primary standards (relating to human health) and secondary standards (relating to human welfare considerations other than health). This is irrational because an environmental improvement gives us benefits that come in many forms, and it is inappropriate to compare some arbitrary subset of benefits to the costs of a policy rather than *all* of the benefits. The distinction between primary and secondary standards should be eliminated.

14

Hedonic Methods of Valuing Environmental Amenities

In the previous chapter, we looked at a common way of inferring the benefits of an environmental policy, namely placing values on the damages that will not occur as a consequence of instituting the policy. For that approach to work well, the causes of the damages that happen to us cannot be well perceived, otherwise we would engage in costly behavior to avoid those damages. In this chapter we consider the implications of a polar opposite assumption regarding perceptions, namely that we have *perfect* perceptions of both a) where it is clean and dirty and b) what various levels of environmental quality mean to our health and welfare. Under these assumptions, we would expect people to attempt to avoid pollution damages. In fact, as long as the marginal cost of avoiding damages is less than the marginal benefits of avoiding damages, we would expect people to continue to avoid damages.

Two ways that people can avoid pollution damages is by locating in cleaner towns or by locating in cleaner parts of a given town. That environmental values can be measured indirectly by the behavior of wages and rents (higher wages and lower rents in dirtier places) has led to this approach being called the hedonic method.[1] We will discuss this method in detail in this chapter, because it is commonly misinterpreted and will be seen to generally result in estimates of environmental values that are downward biased.

The fundamental notion underlying the hedonic methods is merely that people like to make themselves as well off as possible (exactly the assumptions that we make about their behavior in ordinary markets). *All other things being equal*, we would all prefer to live in a cleaner town or live in a cleaner part of a town. The idea with hedonic methods is to examine how much households are willing to pay in land or labor markets to live in cleaner locations, because they will in general *have* to pay, as we shall see. The main ideas are really quite simple, but to gain a clear understanding of this method we shall first consider rent and wage compensation separately, and then develop an integrated model that will be useful for concerns extending far beyond interests in the environment. Because we are all members of some household, let us take up the land market first.

HEDONIC METHODS: PROPERTY VALUE OR RENT COMPENSATION

Consider the case of rents or property values within a given town, say the town you grew up in.[2] What determines how much a house will sell or rent for? Clearly this will be related to the nature of the traits that the house possesses. Some of those traits are structural, such as whether it is constructed from stone or wood, square footage, number of bathrooms, size of lot, presence of pool or tennis court, type of heat, and so on. However, when one hears real estate agents saying house values are determined by three things (location, location, location) they are focusing on neighborhood traits, such as school quality, freedom from crime, access (to shopping, oceans, universities, central business districts), and so on. These traits are location-fixed public goods whose prices end up being bundled together into the price of the house along with the structural traits.[3] Environmental quality is, viewed from this perspective, just another location-fixed trait that is desirable from a household's perspective.

Assuming perceptions are perfect and that we have a competitive housing market, the value of clean air gets paid for; there is no such thing as a free lunch in amenities, any more than you can buy a house with a second bedroom for the same amount as a house without that trait. If we can determine how much people are willing to pay for an otherwise identical home in a clean location versus a dirty location, we will have a measure of exactly what we want—the marginal dollar willingness to pay for environmental quality—which can then be compared to the dollar marginal cost of environmental quality.

The process runs as follows:

1. First, obtain as much information as possible about the traits—structural, neighborhood, and environmental quality—of all houses (in what is hopefully a large sample), along with their property values or contract rent. In an ideal world, the property value (the dependent variable) would be the actual sales price, but sometimes information

is used from multiple-listing books, scaled up or down by the going ratio of list price to exchange price.

2. Next, perform a so-called regression analysis that statistically relates the property value (dependent variable) to its determinants (the independent variables associated with structure or neighborhood). Note that this examination involves many possible functional forms and that nonlinearities, synergisms, and such may be important.[4] That there is little theoretical guidance on the nature of the relationship between property values and their determinants presents problems, and sometimes enables advocates to publish different conclusions from *identical* raw data.[5]

3. The coefficients on the environmental quality variables reveal how much impact a given change in environmental quality has on property values for average households.[6] That is, the trade-off between environmental quality and other goods can be directly measured. Because higher environmental quality is a desired trait of a house, we expect to observe *higher* house prices or rents in cleaner areas, all other things being equal.

There are several problems with the property value studies, stemming either from data limitations or from the assumption of perfect information. If some other amenities are positively correlated with the environmental measure, *and* those other amenities are omitted from the equation, the value of the environment will to be overstated. For example, suppose that the less polluted parts of a city are also more desirable for several other reasons (less crime, better schools, less graffiti, better streets, better lighting, more parks, and so on), and some of these other goods are not included in the equation. By not including the other goods that are correlated with environmental quality, the impact of environmental quality will seem to be larger than it is, because the effects of the other variables not included will be at least partially attributed to environmental quality.[7] For a variety of reasons (e.g., that the cleaner parts of a city tend to be occupied by richer people) one would expect other spatially varying traits (e.g., school quality) to be positively correlated with environmental quality. With constantly improving data collection, this problem will become less important over time.

But, on the other hand, suppose that people do not fully perceive the impact of pollution on their health and well-being or how the pollution levels vary across locations or both. This is quite plausible, because even the "experts" have widely varying opinions about the amount of damage stemming from pollution (see discussion of SSD in chapter 13). Moreover, because many pollutants are odorless, colorless, and tasteless in ambient concentrations commonly encountered, it might be difficult for the average person to even know whether a particular house is in an area that is high or low in pollution. If buyers do not properly perceive all of the damages from pollution or if they cannot tell which locations are dirtier, the benefits estimated by this approach will be understated. People will not pay for something that cannot offer them tangible benefits.

What is the net effect of these potential biases, one suggesting overvaluation, and one suggesting undervaluation? Nobody knows with great certainty, although we shall take this up in greater detail in closing. Many studies, however, show strong positive relationships between property values and environmental quality. The property value approach is particularly useful for valuing spatially concentrated environmental damages, for example the impact of toxic waste dumps on surrounding land values. As we shall see, however, sorting out the likely direction of bias is more complicated than it seems to this point.

HEDONIC METHODS: WAGE COMPENSATION

A quite similar technique approaches the hedonic valuation of environmental quality by looking at labor markets rather than land markets. The idea is that some labor market regions are more polluted than others and that people will have to be compensated for the pollution they experience to be willing to work in dirtier cities. That is, if City A (one of two otherwise identical cities) has higher pollution levels than City B, residents would move from A to B, reducing the labor supply in A (raising wages) while increasing the labor supply in B (lowering wages). The movements would continue to occur until the wage differential just compensated people for the higher pollution in City A. Again, if this approach seems plausible, it has the desirable feature of getting exactly what we want—the marginal willingness to pay in dollar terms—which can then be compared to the marginal costs of policies yielding that amount of cleanness.

The process for the wage compensation approach runs as follows:

1. First, obtain as much data as possible on the determinants of wages for people at various locations (education, experience, age, occupation, region, and so on) and their wages along with measures of environmental quality levels in those locations.
2. Next, perform a regression analysis that statistically relates the wage (as the dependent variable) to its determinants (the independent variables already discussed). As noted for property values, there is little guidance on functional form (degree of linearity, interactions among variables, and so on), offering the possibility that advocates will distort the information by their choices.

3. The coefficients on the environmental quality variable will indicate how much impact a given change in environmental quality has on wages, holding constant other wage determinants. As with the property value approach, the trade-offs between environmental goods and other goods that people also value can be directly measured. Because higher levels of environmental quality are a desirable trait of a labor market area, we would expect that wages would be *lower* in the locations with high environmental quality because the supply of labor would be greater to such areas.

As was the case for property value studies, environmental values generated in this way can either overstate or understate true values. Omitted other goods that are positively correlated with environmental quality, as for example the presence of an ocean or a symphony orchestra, would tend to overstate the value of environmental quality. Oppositely, if environmental quality differences across labor market regions are not perceived or if people do not know how environmental quality affects them, the true benefits of cleaning up will be understated by this method. As with property values, however, a large number of wage studies indicate that environmental quality does matter to people; they are willing to give up wages to live in cleaner locations.

WAGE AND PROPERTY VALUE
DIFFERENTIALS ARE NOT ALTERNATIVES

Until fairly recently, the preceding hedonic approaches to valuing environmental improvements were viewed as alternative approaches.[8] That is, it was thought that one could find out what clean air was worth *either* by examining property value variation in land markets or by examining wage variation in labor markets. The approaches were viewed as alternative ways of measuring the same environmental preferences. Indeed, if the values happened to be similar under the two methods, greater confidence was placed in either as a measure.

It turns out that this is incorrect under plausible assumptions about peoples' behavior when evaluating locations. Indeed, for this view to be valid, it must be the case that people follow a two-stage procedure in picking a location. First, only looking at wages (and average pollution levels), they decide among alternative labor markets; only then, having settled on a labor market, do they select a location based on housing price (and pollution) variation within that area. Yet clearly one would do much better in general to look at the combination of wages, rents, and amenities available prior to selecting a location.

Another way to think about this is that, between two otherwise identical locations, the one that is more polluted will be less attractive, so, people will move from the location that is more polluted to the location that is less polluted until they are equally well off in both locations. But as they move into the location that is less polluted they both increase the supply of labor (driving down wages) and increase the demand for land (driving up rents). Hence, the true value of the locations that are less polluted is the *sum* of what is being paid for reduced pollution in both the labor and land markets.[9]

A GRAPHICAL EXPOSITION OF THE HEDONIC METHOD

Imagine, initially, that the entire world were a flat, featureless plain, where all locations are literally *identical*. There is no variation in closeness to ocean, scenic views, and so on. There would be no reason to pay more for one location than for another. Moreover, imagine—again initially (we will be dropping these restrictive assumptions shortly)—that all households have the same preferences and all firms have the same profit functions. In particular, there is no variation in desires for lot size or income by households and no variation in the land or labor intensity of production processes. This case is depicted in figure 14.1.

The upward sloping curve, labeled V, represents rent and wage combinations that would be equally attractive to households—that is, if rents are

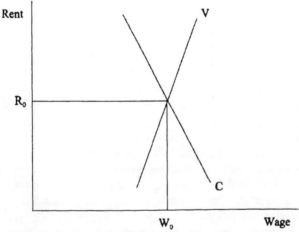

Figure 14.1. Equilibrium rent and wage, when there is no amenity variation

higher in one location than another, residents at that location would have to be compensated by a higher wage there. If wages were not higher residents would be worse off in the city with high rents and would leave, driving down rents. With no variation in amenities, higher rents would have to be compensated for by higher wages.[10]

Similarly, from the firm's perspective, because there is no variation in amenities that affect productivity over space (no deep water ports or differential access to mine mouths), if rents were higher in a location, wages would have to be lower. If wages were not lower in some location, firms would be less profitable there and would leave, lowering labor demand and causing wages to fall.

In such an incredibly boring world, we would observe identical rent levels and wage rates in all locations. If a location offered any wage/rent combination not at the intersection of the V and C curves in figure 14.1, it must be the case that either firms or households are better off or worse off at that location, a nonsustainable situation.

If, for example, a location offered R_0 rents but a wage rate that was greater than W_0, households would be better off at that location, while firms would be worse off at that location. Households would enter (increasing the supply of labor) and firms would exit (decreasing the demand for labor) and wages would fall. Firms leaving would cause rents to fall and households entering would cause rents to rise, as the wages fall. Whether rents rise or fall during the movement to equilibrium depends on whether households move in faster than firms move out. But, in a true equilibrium, satisfaction must be the same everywhere or people will move, and profits must be the same everywhere or firms will move. If there is no variation in amenities that affect households or firms, rents and wages will become equal in all locations.

Now let us begin dropping these unrealistic assumptions, first by introducing variation in an amenity that households care about, but which does not affect firm profitability at all. Perhaps a scenic view comes into existence at one location, or one location becomes sunnier or has lower humidity than other locations. What will happen? With initial wages and rents the same everywhere, the nicer location offers a higher level of satisfaction, so households would be expected to migrate to it. The influx of households will raise the demand for land (increasing rents) and increase the supply of labor (lowering wages). Indeed, households would continue to enter until the wage decreases and rent increases rendered the nicer location no nicer than elsewhere—in other words, they would enter until the lower wages and higher rents exactly compensated for the nicer amenities.[11]

This case is depicted in figure 14.2, where the dashed V_1 curve shows the wage and rent combinations that would make households just as well off in the nice location as in other less-nice locations.[12] That is, with the higher

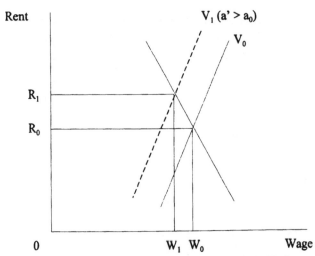

Figure 14.2.   Wage and rent compensation for a desirable household amenity

level of amenity, a′, in the nice place, households will move into that place until the increase in rents $(R_1 - R_0)$ *and* decrease in wages $(W_1 - W_0)$ just exactly compensate households for the niceness of the location. It should now be clear that treating rent hedonic compensation and wage hedonic compensation estimates as alternatives is incorrect; to accurately measure the value of the amenity, the wage and rent compensation must be added together.

Further clarifying, in light of figure 14.2, a rent hedonic equation would indicate that the value of the amenity was only $(R_1 - R_0)$, when—if all compensation occurred in the housing market—the true value of the amenity would be the much larger entire vertical distance from R_1 to the original V_0 curve. Similarly, a wage hedonic would suggest that the value of the amenity was only $(W_1 - W_0)$ when the true value is the much larger horizontal distance from the V_0 curve to the V_1 curve. It is tempting to say that the nice city has a higher cost of living, but that is misleading. It actually has a higher benefit of living, and competitive bidding in land and labor markets for those benefits forces households to pay for the benefits.

If some location trait is a *disamenity* to households, and is neutral to firms, the preceding discussion merely reverses all signs. Households must be compensated for the disamenity via some mix of higher wages or lower rents, with the V curve shifting to the right rather than to the left. It might be useful to graph this case and ponder it.

But there can be amenities for firms as well as households. How does that work? If a location is more productive for some reason, firms seeking profits would want to move into that location to make greater profits. In fact, rational firms would move to the more productive location as long as they can achieve higher profits by doing so. But as they move in, they increase the demand for labor, driving up wages, and they directly drive up industrial rents (and indirectly drive up residential rents, as we shall see). Eventually, these higher labor and land costs will offset the dollar value of the amenity that enhances productivity.

The situation is shown in figure 14.3, which is similar to the previous figure except that now the amenity affects only the firm, whereas in figure 14.2 it was only the household that was affected by the amenity. As firms move into the location that is desirable for them, perhaps because of a deep water port or nearness to a raw material, they will drive up both rents and wages. They will continue to move into the productive location until its productivity is completely offset by the higher prices that must be paid for land and labor.

Note that even though rents have gone up to households, they are no worse off than before. This is because they are being compensated for the higher rents by the higher wages that they receive in equilibrium. In this case, because the location is not nicer from the household's perspective, the higher rents *do* represent a higher cost of living, but one that is completely offset by higher wages. Households' real satisfactions are unaffected by the presence of the firm amenity. While not of great importance for purposes of this book, the value of the amenity to the firms could also be calculated as the sum of what they are paying for it in the land and labor markets.

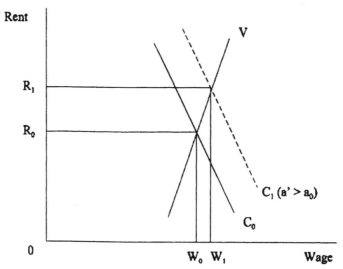

Figure 14.3. **Wage and rent compensation for a desirable firm amenity**

As with the household, if a location-specific trait is a *disamenity* to firms they would require compensation in the form of some mix of lower rents or lower wages. Firms would exit the location until that compensation made the undesirable area as profitable as other locations.

The real world is not so cut-and-dried as the two preceding extreme cases would suggest. Sometimes an amenity from a household's perspective will be a disamenity from the firm's perspective and vice versa. Or an amenity for a household might also be an amenity for a firm (e.g., a deep water port that offers transportation savings and recreational benefits). We shall consider one case of particular relevance to environmental economics.

Suppose that a location passes a law that forces firms to clean up pollution. This will make the location less desirable to a firm due to the higher production costs associated with the pollution controls. But the law will result in a cleaner environment, which will make the location more desirable to households. What will happen in this case? Because firms will be leaving one would expect both rents and wages to fall, but because households will enter the more attractive area, one would expect rents to rise and wages to fall. Wages will clearly fall (because both effects work in the same direction), but the effect on rents is in general ambiguous. We do not know—without further information about how desirable the clean air is to people or how undesirable the cost effect is to firms—which effect dominates. The city might get larger (if firm cost impacts of the law are negligible and households greatly value the environment) or it might get smaller (if cost impacts of the law are large and environmental benefits are small).

This case is depicted in figure 14.4, where I have drawn the effects as offsetting from the perspective of city size. For this specific case, it turns out that the full benefits of cleaning up the air are captured in wages, with no changes in property values or rents. This would, of course, be a fluke in the sense that there would generally be rent effects, positive or negative.[13] The point is that without more information about whether the amenity is more important to firms or to households, the impact on rents is ambiguous.

When the amenity at a location is good for both households and firms, both would want to move in. This situation would cause rents to unambiguously rise (because both households and firms are moving in, increasing the demand for land), while the wage effect is ambiguous; firms moving in demanding labor would tend to drive wages up, but households moving in supplying labor would tend to drive wages down. Again, the net effect would depend on whether the amenity is more important to firms than to households (i.e., would depend on which curve shifts up the most in the graphical setting). In this case, the value of the amenity will appear largely in land markets, but again only as a fluke would there be no labor market effects.

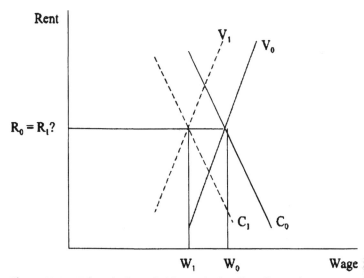

Figure 14.4.   When the household amenity is a firm disamenity

The various possibilities are shown in table 14.1, recognizing that a trait that is location specific may have a neutral effect or be desirable or be undesirable for either households or firms. It would be a useful exercise to draw the graphs associated with each case.

While the graphs and table might seem complicated, on further reflection what is going on is simple. If a location offers a trait that is desirable to firms, all other things being equal, they will move in, driving up both wages and rents until that location is no more desirable than anywhere else, and conversely (e.g., R up and W up, relative to elsewhere). If a location offers a trait that is desirable to households, all other things being equal, they will move in, driving down wages and driving up rents until that location is no more desirable than anywhere else, and conversely (e.g., R up and W down, relative to elsewhere). All the various possibilities of table 14.1 are just combinations of these possibilities.

Table 14.1. The Possible Effects of an Amenity on Households and Firms

Households/Firms	Desirable to firms	Neutral to firms	Undesirable to firms
Desirable to households	$R > R_0$, W?	$R > R_0$, $W < W_0$	R?, $W < W_0$
Neutral to households	$R > R_0$, $W > W_0$	Base case scenario, R_0 and W_0	$R < R_0$, $W < W_0$
Undesirable to households	R?, $W > W_0$	$R < R_0$, $W > W_0$	$R < R_0$, W?

We have assumed that households and firms are all identical in the preceding discussion. This is of course not the case. Land-intensive firms would not be expected to be found in locations where land is expensive (which is why corn is not seen growing in downtown New York). Similarly, those households that have unusually large preferences for land (e.g., households with large families) would not locate where land is expensive.

If a firm's labor demands are unusually large, it would avoid locations with unusually high wages. If a household does not supply labor (e.g., the retired[14]), they would want to locate where amenities are mostly paid for in wages rather than rents. This would also be the case for those who have high demand for services. Conversely, those households that supply low skilled labor to service industries are likely to be "priced out" of desirable and *high rent* locations (e.g., Malibu, California, Aspen, Colorado, or Key West, Florida) and will have to be compensated in higher wages to locate there or commute in to work; that is, the low skilled labor will actually have *higher* wages in desirable locations.

As the preceding makes clear—and as even casual reference to the real world verifies—there is a rich tapestry of locational choices when the full implications of the role of firm and household amenities are considered. This is even more the case when endogenous amenities are considered, amenities such as the amount of other people "like me" are present in a community (e.g., the ethnic neighborhoods of large cities that often make them much more attractive to particular types of people than would otherwise be the case).

Turning specifically to environmental concerns of bias in the use of the hedonic method to value environmental projects affecting households there are several issues to ponder. In early property value and wage compensation studies data limitations or carelessness often resulted in the omission of many variables, other than pollution, that affect household welfare. This would not be a problem if the omitted variables were uncorrelated with the pollution variables of interest (their omission would just add white noise, reducing the precision with which property values or wages were explained but not biasing the environmental coefficients). But in many cases one would expect other goods to be correlated with environmental quality; that is, one might expect environmental quality to be higher in suburbs than in central cities. Suburbs, however, are also likely to have better schools and lower crime than central cities. If school quality or safety are omitted from the equation, the environmental variable will pick up their effects, with *overstatement* of the value we place on environmental quality.[15] Similarly, in wage studies, climate amenities might well be correlated with pollution (i.e., the "Rustbelt" industrial areas are generally both more polluted and less desirable climatically than the "Sunbelt"; hence wages in the Sunbelt will be lower for both reasons, and failing to include climate variables will result in overstatment of the value placed on environmental quality). At one point, this was a major concern, but the past two decades have seen far better data availability and data analysis.[16]

There are three major reasons why it seems clear that hedonic methods *understate* the value of environmental quality improvements. The first, and most obviously damaging, is that the benefits of environmental quality must be *fully perceived* by households for them to be willing to pay more for cleaner locations. Even the world's foremost health experts have spirited debates about the role various pollutants play in human disease and death. It seems implausible that somehow ordinary people would accurately perceive such things; moreover, because many pollutants are odorless, colorless, and tasteless in normal ambient concentrations, it is unlikely that ordinary people know where the clean places even are.

Why do hedonic studies show such large environmental effects then? It is certainly the case that people *will* perceive localized smells, bad visibility, and other impacts of pollution that can be readily sensed by humanity. Yet it is precisely such perceived damages that are *ignored* in the SSD approach discussed in the previous chapter. That chapter invoked the assumption that damages (typically health damages) were *unperceived* and just occurred to people at greater rates in dirtier locations. Yet it is commonly viewed as a good corroborative thing when estimates from hedonic studies show damages of the same or nearly the same magnitude as those from SSD studies.

But they *cannot be alternatives*. A much stronger case can be made for *adding* together the damages estimated from an SSD study to those of an hedonic study to get the true damages, those both perceived and unperceived. There might well be some double counting, because an area that is unhealthy might also smell bad; but it is likely that the two methods pick up largely unrelated damage categories, those perceivable and those that are not perceivable by households. This point is quite important in practical environmental situations, whether in regulatory rulings or in court testimony. The benefits of environmental cleanup are estimated *either* from SSD types of approaches or hedonic types of approaches, but the estimates are never added together, which would in many cases double the estimated damages.

Moreover, each of the damage estimation methodologies separately understates damages as typically conducted. SSD, as summarized in the previous chapter, tends to omit minor health effects (e.g., watery eyes) and emphasizes acute damages rather than the more difficult to study chronic damages. And it is the case that expert legal/regulatory hedonic testimony still typically employs *either* a property value study or a wage study, despite our having known for more than two decades that compensation for environmental damages will generally occur in *both* the land and labor markets as discussed in detail in this chapter. The extent to which damages appear in land versus labor markets would generally vary according to many things,[17] but considering either market separately is likely to greatly underestimate the damages from pollution.

The final reason why hedonic methods might be expected to understate the benefits of environmental cleanup stems from the relative supplies of clean locations relative to the relative demands for clean locations. Referring to the discussion of consumer surplus in chapter 2, the hedonic method results in *zero* spatial consumer surplus. That is, if one location is nicer than another location, households will continue to move to the nicer location until it is no longer nicer. There will be no consumer surplus over space, and indeed this is one of the reasons the hedonic method is desirable in that you can get the *full* benefits that are perceived.

But, the fact that people are different means that understatement of environmental benefits (damage reduction) can occur if there are more locations with the amenity than there are people strongly desiring the amenity. Suppose, for example, that there are few households containing really sick individuals, individuals with weakened cardiopulmonary systems who would be highly damaged by pollution. Such households might be *willing* to pay a lot for a clean location, but they might only *have* to pay a much smaller amount, if the number of clean locations is large relative to the number of these households. They will get, in other words, consumers' surplus over space. Inferring the value of cleaning up the environment from the average person in this case would ignore the high benefits received by these households.[18]

The policy implication of this chapter is that efforts to value environmental (and other) amenities via hedonic methods are flawed and result in bias against the value of cleaning up the environment. The perceptions issue is at the heart of the flaw, but it is also the case that treating land market analyses and labor market analyses as alternatives is an important source of downward environmental bias in practice. One of the reasons for the popularity of this method is that the benefits of an environmental project that improves the environment come in convenient units that are dollar denominated that make it convenient to compare them to the costs of the project. But convenience per se is of little consequence when it comes along with bias, bias that strongly suggests that the environment is being undervalued.

QUESTIONS FOR DISCUSSION

1. What effects of environmental quality do you think are perceived versus unperceived?
2. Do you know which parts of the city you grew up in are clean and which parts are dirty? If you are aware of which locations are clean and which are dirty, how much would you pay in higher property values to live in the clean locations?

3. Suppose that you enter the job market and are considering jobs in two or more locations. How important will environmental quality be in your decision? How much wage compensation would be necessary to get you to move to a fairly dirty city? Would the answer to that question depend on how many clean areas—if any—there were in the city that was dirty overall? How is that answer affected if the clean areas are quite expensive?

4. Are hedonic methods picking up use values or nonuse values? Are there ever any exceptions to your answer to this question? (Hint: Would Warren Buffett, Ted Turner, or Bill Gates always answer the same as you?)

5. Why was it argued that wage compensation for amenities and rent/property value compensation for amenities should be added together?

6. Which do you feel is more likely to result in the greater error, adding the benefits from hedonic analyses to those of the SSD method or using one of them separately? Would your answer to this question depend on the nature of the environmental good being considered? (Hint: if a pollutant is odorless, colorless, and tasteless would its health damages be picked up by the hedonic method? If it smells but is harmless, would its aesthetic damages be picked up by the SSD method?)

7. Suppose that what can be perceived about pollution and what cannot be perceived are positively correlated. That is, suppose that unhealthy locations also generally smell bad. Does that correlation matter to your answer to question 6? Or what if the unhealthy locations generally smell bad, but only the experts know what the correlation is? What happens to your answer to question 6 if households are assumed to make some assumption about what the correlation is (e.g., they might assume perfect correlation of one or zero correlation or something in between)?

8. When would there be zero spatial variation in consumer surplus? (Hint: When you are thinking about taking a job in a different location, would you rather be like everyone else, or do you have unusual preferences?)

9. Which do you think is likely to be more important, omitted variable bias (leaving variables out of the hedonic equation that are positively correlated with the environmental variable of interest) or failure to properly perceive spatial variation in environmental quality?

10. There were many complicated graphs in this chapter. But is not the essence of the argument simple? (Hint: If a place is nicer for a firm, what will happen to wages and rents? If worse for a firm? If it is nicer to households? Worse? Are not all locations some combination of these four possibilities?)

NOTES

1. The hedonic method, which means literally *doctrine of pleasure*, has its origins in the late 1930s when Andrew Court who worked for General Motors wanted to know what various automobile traits (e.g., weight, horsepower, gas mileage, paint color, and so on) were worth to people. One way to determine what the traits of a car are worth is to look at how used car prices vary with the various traits of interest. For example, statistically holding constant horsepower, size, color, model, and so on the impact of the presence of an automatic transmission or power steering would be reflected in higher prices for cars possessing that trait (assuming that people prefer the presence of the trait).

2. Most studies are actually conducted with property values, but there will be similar relationships between either rents or property values and various amenities for either measure. We will use both terms interchangeably.

3. Note that the location specificity essentially transforms such public goods into private goods bought in a housing bundle.

4. One might generally expect marginal damages to be an increasing function of the level of pollution, and this can be readily tested for by putting in quadratic terms, using logarithms, and so on. And a so-called interaction term can explore whether the damages from, say, sulfur oxides depend synergistically on the amount of fine particulate present.

5. See R. Krumm and P. Graves, "Morbidity and Pollution," *Journal of Environmental Economics and Management* 9, no. 4 (December 1982): 311–27, for an application to air quality of a methodology designed to eliminate biases when theoretical guidance on functional form is limited.

6. While beyond the scope of this book, a second stage in this analysis can reveal how individual demands for location-fixed amenities vary by income, family size, and other individual-specific variables. In other words, information can be obtained on the underlying preferences that gave rise to the observed market relationship between environmental quality and property values.

7. The environmental quality coefficient will appear to be larger by the effect on property values associated with the omitted variable *times* the (positive) correlation of that variable with environmental quality.

8. For virtually any new theoretical observation, it takes about two decades for that observation to be operationalized by politicians and practitioners.

9. There are many Rand-McNally *Places Rated* almanacs that rank cities according to quality of life. The approach taken is to focus on some number of traits (parks, school quality, crime, and so on) assigning a number from 1 to 5, with higher numbers being better. The numbers are added up and the city with the highest number is said to be best. There are many problems with this approach (notably, it weights all traits equally, when people would presumably care much more about some traits than others). Also, and interestingly, under this approach, high rents and property values are usually taken to be a bad thing and result in a lower ranking (e.g., in one such study, Newark, New Jersey, ranked much higher than Santa Barbara, California, in large part because of the higher cost of living in Santa Barbara; but of course it was not a higher cost of living but rather a higher benefit of living, a benefit that we just have to pay for). The economic approach merely argues that the more we are

willing to pay for the traits associated with a location, the better that location must be. For a well-conducted economic study, see G. C. Blomquist, M.C. Berger, and J.P. Hoehn, "New Estimates of the Quality of Life in Urban Areas," *American Economic Review* 78 (1988): 89–107.

10. Technically the V curve is the locus of all wage-rent combinations that give exactly the same level of satisfaction. Normally, goods (public or private) are presumed to be what enters household utility, and we assume that more goods are preferred to less and that more leisure is preferred to less. The V curve stems from something called an indirect utility function, because it is written in terms of prices rather than goods. Higher prices for goods (rents) are bad and higher prices for labor (wages) are good. Similarly, the C curve is the locus of wage-rent combinations that give exactly the same level of unit costs, which corresponds to profits for a good sold on national markets with low shipping costs.

11. Two things should be noted. First, as people enter they might also lower levels of endogenous disamenities (e.g., air pollution, congestion) along with raising rents and lowering wages. As long as all amenity variables are included in the analysis this is not a problem, because the "net niceness" of the city will still be captured by rents and wages. Second, it might not take too many people actually moving to result in full compensation for the city's niceness. This is akin to the fact that only a few drivers need to move from slow lanes to fast lanes on the freeway at rush hour to make all lanes equally fast.

12. The set of V curves, for various amenity levels, are called level sets, because they all give the same level of satisfaction in equilibrium.

13. The shares of compensation for an amenity are not bounded by zero or one when both households and firms are affected, so it would be theoretically possible, though unlikely in practice, that a single market hedonic approach could overstate the benefits of cleanup.

14. The retired would be expected to move to locations where relatively more of the amenity value is capitalized into wages, because retirees would be able to get a free lunch, not having to pay for amenities in this case (for greater detail, see P. Graves and D. Waldman, "Multimarket Amenity Compensation and the Behavior of the Elderly," *American Economic Review* 81, no. 5 (December 1991): 1374–81).

15. The bias on the coefficient of environmental quality variable would be equal to the effect of the omitted variable on property value (or wage) times the correlation of that variable with environmental quality in the data. If the correlation is small, the bias would be small, even with important omitted variables; similarly, if the correlation is high (closer to one), then the full effect of any omitted variable would be attributed to environmental quality.

16. GIS modeling enables the merging of many disparate data sets, while use of something called fixed effects modeling (where dummy variables, taking on the value 1 or 0 if an observation is or is not in a specific location, implicitly holds constant a host of unmeasured variables).

17. If an environmental pollutant were highly concentrated (e.g., a hazardous waste dump) one would expect a greater percentage of its damage to appear in property values, while the damages from more regionally ubiquitous pollutants might be expected to appear primarily in wage rates. The existence of firm amenities and disamenities complicates the generation of firm conclusions, but using only one of the

two markets that environmental quality is valued in must generally lead to understatement of damages.

18. As an illustration of the possible/occasional importance of this point, suppose that a large city, based on a hedonic analysis suggesting that its mass transit system has low benefits, is considering dropping that costly system. Handicapped individuals might be receiving extremely large benefits from that transit system, but because they are small in number their values of access to the transit system are not picked up in the hedonic analysis. Similarly, for a city contemplating the addition of a mass transit system, the high demands of the handicapped might not be properly considered. This point does not really deserve great emphasis, however, for benefit-cost analysis of *increments* to existing systems, because the *marginal* benefits to the high demanders will be near zero, despite high total benefits (which include consumer surplus). Illustrating further, it is only at rush hour when those desiring to travel at high rates of speed are particularly harmed and have high marginal benefits for an additional lane relative to typical drivers. During normal traffic flow periods, when everyone can travel at the speed they wish, the consumer surplus received by the speeders has no bearing on the marginal benefits of adding a lane. The marginal benefit of an incremental lane is zero when everyone can travel at any speed they wish. The hedonic method is like rush hour in that it assumes there are fewer desirable fast lanes than there are people wanting fast lanes, and movement among lanes occurs to make all lanes equally desirable.

15

Travel Cost Method of Valuing Environmental Amenities

In previous chapters we have discussed approaches to environmental valuation that directly construct markets (contingent valuation or voting) or indirectly reveal values via observed willingness to pay for related goods (e.g., SSD or hedonics). The travel cost method is another indirect measure that is useful in certain circumstances but which has flaws from both an economist's and an environmentalist's perspective.

The central theoretical flaw in the travel cost method, in common with SSD and hedonics, is that it can only capture use values, shedding no light on nonuse (or passive) values, which could be much larger, at least in principle. Moreover, there are two additional flaws that are likely to result in overstatement of use value, further distorting resource allocation against nonuse outcomes. Other flaws will be discussed in closing.

The travel cost method is typically used to value sites that are used for recreation, though it can be used for any destination that is visited as an amenity. The method can assign values (including consumer surplus, not just marginal willingness to pay) to be placed on the elimination of a site or the creation of a new site. In some applications it can also be used to value a change in the environmental quality at a recreational site.

How does the travel cost method work? The fundamental idea is that the number of trips a household makes to a recreational site in a given time period is analogous to the number of pounds of broccoli purchased in a given time period. Just as the number of pounds of broccoli purchased will increase at a lower price and decrease at a higher price, the number of trips to the recreational area will increase if it has a lower price.

But what is the price paid for a recreational site? The price is the time and travel cost expenses (along with any entry fee) that are incurred during a visit to the recreational site. If people travel a long distance to get to the site (facing a high price) they would be expected to take fewer trips per year to the site than those living nearby (facing a low price).[1] Suppose, for example, that gasoline is $3.00 per gallon and an individual earns a wage of $20 per hour at work (after taxes).[2] If gas mileage is 25 miles to the gallon—at an assumed average speed of 50 miles per hour—and if the individual lives 50 miles away from the recreational site, the cost of the round trip to the site is $12.00 (four gallons of gas) plus $40.00 (two hours of time) or $52.00. Suppose such an individual takes two trips a year to the recreational site.

Another individual, facing the same price for gas and average speed to the site, might have a lower wage of $15 per hour and might live 25 miles from the recreational site. For this individual, the price of a round trip to the recreational site is $6.00 (two gallons of gas) plus $15.00 (one hour of time) or $21.00. This individual would be expected, all other things being equal, to take more frequent trips to the recreational site, say five trips per year.

A recreational site will have many such individual visitors, the two above being depicted on the overall demand curve for trips to the site shown in figure 15.1.[3] What is the value of this recreational site? The value, as always, is the area under the demand curve in the figure. As an illustration of how this information might be used in a practical policy setting, suppose that this recreational area is being considered for elimination, to be replaced by a shooting range for a local gun club. The shooting range will, itself, have alternative locations that could be selected. Suppose that the net value of

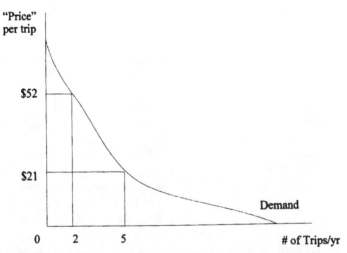

Figure 15.1.   Valuing a recreational site by the travel cost method

having the shooting range at the location of the recreational site versus some alternative location is $10,000. If the area under the demand curve of figure 15.1 exceeds $10,000, the location is more valuable left as a recreational area than converted into a shooting range, and conversely.[4]

The travel cost method is simple, not terribly controversial, and has a great deal of appeal to many people, because it is based on actual behavior. Moreover, this method can often be conducted at fairly low cost, with the necessary information readily available through surveys of visitors.[5] Simple zones (perhaps defined by zip codes of visitors), at varying distances from the recreation site can be created and merged with information collected from visitors about the number of visits they make (trips purchased) and which zone they live in (different prices). Or one could use an individual travel cost approach, using more detailed surveys of the actual travel costs of those visiting the recreational site under consideration.[6] Such analyses should hold constant socio-demographic variables, such as age, income, gender, and education levels (either individually or by zone), to obtain true estimates of the impact of price on the quantity of trips.

There are, however, a number of caveats to bear in mind when using the travel cost method. It assumes that individuals respond to changes in explicit travel costs (e.g., $0.35 per mile) as they do to implicit travel costs (time) and also just as they would to changes in admission price (indeed, the three categories are all lumped together).

A more important limitation is that the method assumes that a trip is single purpose. This is often not the case. For example, virtually anyone who visits Devil's Tower in northeastern Wyoming would also visit Mount Rushmore in the nearby Black Hills of South Dakota. It is difficult to apportion the cost of the whole trip to the subcomponent sites. Yet failing to do so (attributing the cost of the whole trip to, say, Devil's Tower) will overstate the value of a single site, perhaps by a great deal.

Similarly, suppose people enjoy travel itself, liking the feeling of being out on the road. In this case the traveler is obtaining those pure travel benefits along with those of the recreational site. This would also result in the overvaluation of the recreational site in question.

As discussed in the first footnote of this chapter, those who value certain sites may choose to live nearby. Essentially, those that have high values are choosing a lower price per trip, something that cannot be done with ordinary private goods. Such people will have low travel costs but high values for the site that are not fully picked up by this method, although the low travel costs will themselves encourage greater trip frequency.[7]

However, the biggest single problem, from an environmentalist's perspective, with the travel cost method is that it cannot be used to measure nonuse values. Employing data from actual users ignores the values that individuals might have for the option to use, as well as bequest values (that might relate to either use or preservation), along with the passive preservation values that could be of great importance in particular settings.

The implications of this discussion for policy are complex. Some recreational or environmental sites will have little in the way of nonuse value associated with them (e.g., a recreational fishing site with little in the way of unique features). The decision to allow a water irrigation project to use the water might be well evaluated using the travel cost method of calculating benefits to compare to the forgone benefits of the irrigation water. But other decisions might involve rare and pristine natural environments (e.g., a decision to allow noisy and polluting snowmobiles in Yellowstone Park, or overnight camping in wilderness areas). For the latter, it is likely that nonuse values will be important. Decisions ignoring those nonuse values, particularly if the use values are overestimated for some of the reasons discussed here, might readily lead to resource misallocation inefficiently harming the environment.

QUESTIONS FOR DISCUSSION

1. Why is the travel cost method only appropriate for valuing use values?
2. Do you think that it is appropriate to treat all categories of cost (explicit out-of-pocket travel costs, implicit time costs, and entry fee, if applicable) as dollar equivalent, or do some categories *mean* more to travelers than others?
3. Some of the concerns associated with the travel cost method would lead to expectations of overvaluation of a site, while others would result in undervaluation. What do you think is the net direction of likely bias?
4. How is taking a trip to a recreational site like the purchase of an ordinary good, say broccoli? How does it differ?

NOTES

1. One difficulty with the travel cost method that differs from the broccoli analogy is that those households with high values for the recreational site can *lower the price they pay for it* by moving closer to the recreational site. This option is not available for broccoli lovers who must face the same price as those who just sort of like broccoli. We shall return to implications of this potential problem in closing.

2. In principle, we want to measure the true opportunity cost of all resources expended during a trip to the recreational site. Ideally, we would know the mileage each visitor's car gets, the depreciation of the car associated with the trip, and their after-tax wage rate. However, the after-tax wage rate is a lower bound estimate of the time cost, because it assumes that people would have chosen to work if they did not

take the trip when they might have chosen to do something else, despite having the option to work. Additionally, salaried individuals also complicate the analysis, with their implicit after-tax wage rate (after tax income divided by the number of hours worked) typically taken as a reasonable proxy for the opportunity cost of time. Some salaried individuals would rather work less (have a higher value of leisure time, hence higher travel cost) while others would rather work more (have a lower value of leisure time, hence lower travel cost).

3. If there is an entrance fee, say $10, some visitors in figure 15.1—those with costs of getting to the site of less than $10—will forgo some of the trips they would have otherwise taken.

4. Sometimes it is easy to make decisions with this method. For example, damming up Hells Canyon (the deepest canyon in North America) to create hydro power was estimated to have economic cost savings over alternative locations of $80,000. Even a low cost and imprecise travel cost survey revealed recreational benefits, that would be lost if the hydro power were pursued, of around $900,000. In public hearings, it was pointed out that even large errors in the benefit analysis would not alter the conclusion not to build the hydro power plant, and that plant was never built, with Congress prohibiting further development of Hells Canyon.

5. As with the survey methods discussed earlier, there are inevitably issues of survey design, selectivity bias, and so on. Moreover, there are data/statistical issues surrounding the estimation of the demand curve for the recreational site that are common to all derivations of market demand curves.

6. While beyond the scope of the present treatment, more complicated so-called random utility approaches can be used, employing survey and other data in more elaborate statistical analyses.

7. It is possible that nearness to the recreation site might cause property values to be higher or wages to be lower, as discussed in the previous chapter. In this eventuality, one could add what is paid in land and labor markets to what is paid in travel costs expended to get to the site to obtain a more accurate estimate of the full value of the site.

16

Political and
Jurisdictional Problems

The preceding several chapters have discussed various approaches to valuing environmental quality improvements, approaches that provide information for use by decision makers in deciding whether the benefits exceed or fall short of the costs of a policy. Throughout that discussion, we have implicitly assumed that those responsible for environmental decision making are at least *attempting* to properly use that information. That is, ignoring important issues of equity, it was presumed that decision makers are interested in maximizing the welfare of the citizens they represent. This implies that all Pareto efficient or Kaldor-Hicks efficient[1] projects would be undertaken to the extent that they could be identified.

There are two important reasons to suspect that those making decisions might not even be particularly interested in pursuing projects that enhance welfare vis-à-vis other projects. Economists, until relatively recently,[2] have naively presumed that politicians would try to correct for any flaws in private markets (would intervene to correct resource misallocations resulting from missing markets). This ignores the incentives that politicians face to pursue their own goals, even when doing so is inconsistent with social welfare. A second source of deliberately faulty decision making stems from the fact that the boundaries of political jurisdictions seldom correspond to the extent of the externality. Decision makers in those jurisdictions will be concerned only with the costs and benefits of a policy for their constituents, even when a policy has substantial benefits accruing outside of that jurisdiction. We shall discuss both problems in some detail, in the following two subsections.

POLITICAL INCENTIVES TO
UNDERVALUE THE ENVIRONMENT

Politicians do not care primarily about efficiency or even equity.[3] What they care about are votes, the votes to get elected (or reelected if they are incumbents). This simple observation has a number of implications and none of them are good news for environmentalists.

The special interest problem has received a great deal of attention in popular and academic writing. The central idea is that when either benefits or costs are concentrated those helped or harmed will go to great lengths to receive those benefits or avoid those costs. As an example of concentrated benefits, the many agricultural subsidy programs greatly help individual farmers, causing groups representing them (e.g., the American Dairy Association) to lobby vigorously on behalf of the programs. The harm from these policies, while greater than the benefits, is spread across hundreds of millions of nonfarmers who pay higher prices for food as well as more taxes than would otherwise be the case. Each nonfarm household is damaged little relative to the concentrated benefits received by farm households.

Of particular relevance for environmentalists is the case where costs are highly concentrated (e.g., costly controls on steel producers, auto producers, cement plants, or dry cleaners) and benefits are widely dispersed, the somewhat improved air quality we all breathe. Representatives of the impacted firms (e.g., National Association of Manufacturers) will have powerful incentives to lobby, contribute to PACs, and so on in an effort to avoid the high and concentrated costs.

One might argue, along the lines of Coase that those harmed by farm policies or helped by environmental policies have interests that will be represented. This is unlikely for a couple of related reasons which, as might be expected, involve transactions costs. First, it is unlikely that representative voters *will even know* about the policies in question. It is fundamentally irrational for voters to be well-informed about any issue that is complicated because to become informed will involve large costs, and the odds of any voter being decisive is vanishingly small. In other words, the costs greatly exceed the benefits of acquiring information relevant for voting (the so-called rational voter ignorance principle). Moreover, as noted, even if a potential voter is informed, his or her vote is unlikely to make a difference in the outcome. Thus, while well-informed voters are more likely to vote than those knowing nothing about the issues, some informed potential voters will not get around to it, aware that their vote is unlikely to make a difference.

A related problem is that one generally votes for candidates rather than directly on specific issues.[4] This means that the voter must accept the bundle of positions that candidates have on a range of issues when voting for them. Frequently, they will like some positions that a candidate holds, while not liking others, and this might be true of the opposition candidate, too. As a consequence, voters might be more-or-less indifferent among candidates, providing yet another rationale for not voting.

Pulling the preceding arguments together, the candidate that is pro-environment a) may not get that message to voters because of rational voter ignorance, b) may have less money for advertising because of smaller PAC contributions, and c) may hold other views that pro-environment voters dislike.

Another political problem is that politicians have short time horizons. Members of the House of Representatives are voted on every two years, the president is elected every four years, and senators are elected every six years. Politicians must then make a difference quickly, which means they will want to deliver benefits as quickly as possible, while deferring costs as long as possible.

In addition to creating a perpetual incentive to run deficits, this incentive distorts the nature of the projects that politicians support. Recall from chapter 3 that the benefits and costs in a properly conducted benefit-cost analysis are appropriately discounted at the opportunity cost of the funds. The projects that politicians are most likely to select for analysis will be expected to have a pattern of benefits and costs that effectively represent a *much larger discount rate*. Most environmental projects involve substantial upfront costs before, often long before (e.g., as with global warming), benefits can be realized. As with the voting paradox discussed in chapter 11, the agenda setter has more power than is commonly supposed and that power is likely to keep environmental projects in the background.

Additionally logrolling (e.g., if you vote for my dam, I'll vote for your airport) tends to encourage too many ordinary projects and too few environmental projects. This is especially so with federal cost sharing in which total benefits may be well below total costs of a project, while *local* benefits might be far in excess of *local* costs. For example, consider a hypothetical dam which might have benefits (in the form of irrigation, flood protection, and electricity generation) to local residents of one billion dollars. If that project had a cost of two billion dollars to local residents, it would of course be rejected. But if the project has federal cost-sharing, say at 80%, the cost to locals will only be $400 million. A project with costs twice benefits will look to the locals trying to get it like it has benefits two-and-a-half times costs.[5] Too many such projects are undertaken. Environmental projects tend not to have properties making them amenable to logrolling; hence they suffer when large deficits result in cost cutting. One might well argue that government does so many things it *should not be doing at all*, that it fails to do the things it should be doing *at all well*.

JURISDICTIONAL INCENTIVES
TO UNDERVALUE THE ENVIRONMENT

Jurisdictional boundaries in the United States and throughout the world tend to be established for historical or geographic reasons. For example, a boundary might be a river separating two states. The nature of the resulting pattern of jurisdictions has extremely important and largely unrecognized negative impacts on political decisions involving the environment. To see how this works, it is instructive to think about what an optimal jurisdiction would be. This, it turns out, is going to depend on what decision is being made. The optimal jurisdiction also depends, as is so often the case, on how one feels about efficiency relative to equity—whose values should count?

For the vast majority of decisions (e.g., decisions involving generation of income and the consumption of ordinary goods), the optimal jurisdiction is the *household*. Each household will decide how much to work to generate the income to buy the goods they wish to buy. Any jurisdiction larger than the household will result in inefficient decisions. If, in other words, somebody other than *you* decides how hard you should work or what you should buy, you are likely to be made worse off (they would be unlikely to select what you would select). It is also the case that, on equity grounds, the household is the preferred jurisdiction, it being generally viewed as unfair for others to decide how much income you should produce or how you should spend your hard-earned dollars. Because you would be worse off, and you are a portion of society, society would be made worse off, too, unless your individual choices result in external damage to others.

But if your actions do result in externalities, who should decide how to modify your behavior? The general answer is that the optimal jurisdiction depends on the extent of the externality.[6] Those who are damaged by the externality would, in an ideal world, be the ones that determine what policy option is chosen, assuming that those damaged cannot pass the costs on to someone else.[7] If a policy has benefits, in terms of reduced damages experienced, that exceed its costs that policy should be pursued, on efficiency grounds.

Concrete examples are useful here. Consider the endangered Chinese panda. It is universally loved and indeed, is more likely to survive because of that. But suppose the decision were entirely up to the Chinese at a time when they are poor and want to use the habitat occupied by the panda? It is true that Coase would likely argue that high Western dollar preservation values for the panda would far exceed the value of the panda habitat to the low-income Chinese. But each person outside of China has an incentive to free ride (as discussed in chapter 7), because each individual's values are likely to be small relative to the amount needed to save the panda. Moreover, the transactions costs of creating a contract to save the panda are high,

even if a large sum of money is generated to save the panda. What would prevent China, a sovereign national jurisdiction, from taking the money to save the panda and then consigning the latter to death by releasing the panda habitat to poor Chinese peasants? The point is that because of transnational jurisdictional problems, it becomes even more likely that the full benefits of an environmental policy do not get counted. In the context of the Coase theorem, jurisdictional sovereignty raises transactions costs.

A different environmental case is provided by the prairie dog. Unlike the panda, the prairie dog (a rodent actually) is *not* universally loved. Prairie dogs are certainly cute furry creatures and most reasonable people would like to see them preserved as a species. To an individual household, however, these creatures are likely to be viewed as pests.[8] Each individual household might want to eradicate *their* prairie dogs while professing an abstract desire to preserve them on somebody *else's* land. What jurisdiction, if any, should make decisions regarding the fate of the prairie dog? Some Western U.S. laws require that prairie dogs can only be relocated with the approval of the county receiving them. This approval is unlikely to be given as a practical matter, because prairie dogs tend to spread rapidly in areas inhabited by humans who have also largely eradicated the prairie dogs' natural predators.

The point of both of the preceding examples is that sometimes good things (actions with benefits greater than costs, such as saving the panda or various whale species) do not happen because of jurisdictional limitations, and bad things (actions with full costs greater than benefits, such as the demise of the prairie dog species) do happen because of jurisdictional limitations.

A great many examples of jurisdictional problems could be discussed. Locating a polluting factory downwind in the jurisdiction housing it might put that factory's pollution in another jurisdiction, while the benefits of having the factory accrue to the home jurisdiction (e.g., jobs, industrial property taxes, and the like). One state, for example Illinois, might have high levels of air pollution that affect nearby Wisconsin, while Wisconsin might have high levels of water pollution that affect nearby Illinois, with neither considering the wishes of the other.

In principle, policies dealing with a) local environmental problems, for example, a control of a waste dump, should be established locally, b) regional environmental problems, for example, acid rain, should be dealt with at the regional level corresponding to the damages, c) national environmental problems, rare in practice, should be dealt with at the national level, and d) transnational environmental problems (e.g., CO_2 buildup, species preservation) should be handled at the transnational level. Unfortunately, at each of the preceding jurisdictional levels decision makers have full sovereignty to decide on the basis of the benefits and costs accruing exclusively in that district.[9]

The jurisdictional problem, then, is that some existing jurisdictions are too small and others are too large. If all damage from a polluter is incurred within a jurisdiction, that jurisdiction will be expected to optimally control the polluter. A larger jurisdiction, for example, national standards for what are local problems, would result in uniform standards when uniformity is inefficient.[10] Generally, however, environmental damages tend to spill over jurisdictional boundaries. This means that residents of a jurisdiction will not be concerned about benefits received by those in other jurisdictions and are likely as a consequence to *undercontrol* polluters.

The incentives facing politicians and the way in which jurisdictions were established both tend to result in decisions that understate the importance of the values that people place on environmental quality. In critiquing benefit-cost analyses, then, environmentalists should be on the lookout for benefits that are omitted by the decision makers (benefits accruing outside of their jurisdiction) or for costs that are overstated by decision makers (because of the power of special interest groups paying those costs).

QUESTIONS FOR DISCUSSION

1. Politicians often claim to care greatly about those electing them. Are the text arguments too cynical in your opinion? Bear in mind, however, that a politician, who is concerned about the welfare of his or her constituents, must get elected to be able to do good things; are the arguments of the political subsection in some sense inevitable?
2. How does the special interest effect work to distort political outcomes? Are special interests always bad? (Hint: recall from previous discussion, that special interests are still values that matter, regardless of the concentration of those values.)
3. Why would you expect logrolling to lead to too many projects undertaken by government? What difference does federal cost sharing make to the power of your argument?
4. Would you expect optimal jurisdictions for environmental problems to bear any relationship at all to actual jurisdictions? There are often special districts, for example, water districts or school districts, that are set up to deal with specific resource allocation issues; should there be special acid rain districts?
5. How do you feel about the loss of sovereignty that would result from special districts such as those from the previous question? Global pollutants (e.g., ozone-depleting CFCs or CO_2 buildup) would require a global jurisdiction; are countries likely to give up their sovereignty to such a district?

NOTES

1. Recall that Pareto efficient projects have the property that one or more people benefit, and *nobody* is harmed, a property of voluntary trades in the absence of externalities. Kaldor-Hicks efficient projects have benefits in excess of costs, hence—at least in principle—can be converted to Pareto efficient projects with transfers from the winners to the losers that leave everyone better off than in the absence of the project.

2. James M. Buchanan received the Nobel Prize in 1986 for his pioneering work in public choice theory (see his "Social Choice, Democracy, and Free Markets," *Journal of Political Economy* LXII (1954): 114–23; "Individual Choice in Voting and the Market," *Journal of Political Economy* LXII (1954): 334–43; and "Positive Economics, Welfare Economics, and Political Economy," *Journal of Law and Economics* II (1959): 124–38.)

3. A more accurate phrasing would be that even if they care a *great deal* about efficiency or equity, they still must get elected to pursue those concerns. So getting elected takes primacy and the need to get elected often ends up causing politicians to compromise their more noble interests.

4. The ubiquitous propositions on the ballot in California are an exception, and such individual initiatives crop up in other locations as well.

5. An analogy here between logrolling and the cost sharing that occurs in restaurants is instructive. It is often taken for granted that the check will be split evenly. As a consequence, each individual diner has an incentive to order more expensive entrees, and they have an incentive to order appetizers and desserts when they ordinarily would not. The reason: If there are five diners, every dollar more they spend on some item only costs them twenty cents. Each has an incentive to overspend, resulting in a much larger than optimal overall check.

6. Recall that the practical value of the Coase theorem hinges on low transactions costs. If some of those damaged occupy a different district, their transactions costs of involvement are large (they are not even voters in the area creating their damages).

7. There is a slight complication here. In principle, even if the costs *are* paid by someone else, as long as the benefits exceed the costs, the policy is efficient, though perhaps inequitable. However, the logrolling example of the previous section makes clear that if the costs can be passed on to others, those experiencing the benefits will want to do so and would be perfectly happy to enact globally inefficient policies as long as the local benefits exceeded the local costs. The issue here is whether, *prior to the decision of what to do*, those harmed think that they can later pass the costs on to someone else (e.g., later bans on night noise from an airport when nearby populations become sufficiently large—through politics, nearby residents might hope to get both access to the airport and quiet, with resulting higher property values).

8. Prairie dogs have fleas that sometimes carry the bubonic plague bacteria, they dig holes that can result in injury to livestock and people, and they munch virtually all edible vegetation, denuding their immediate area.

9. To better clarify the environmental issues, consider the case of legal or illegal low skilled immigration into the United States or other countries. Assume, for

simplicity of argument, that all social welfare programs are only available to citizens and that all migrants spoke English. In such a situation, on efficiency grounds, typical households are almost certainly better off with more immigrants (they raise the return to capital and to high skilled labor, they raise the demand for existing land owned domestically, they lower the cost of goods and services employing them, and so on). On equity grounds, it is evidently the case that they hurt people of low skill, particularly people of the same ethnic groups who immigrated to the United States prior to them. So relatively poor people in the United States are harmed by immigrants whether legal or not. But taking a broader jurisdictional perspective, efforts to limit immigration reduce the ability of the world's truly poor to better themselves while protecting *relatively* rich domestic households.

10. In many respects, national environmental standards are like national nutritional standards, imposing a particular healthful diet on all citizens. Because both individual costs (e.g., the cost of fresh fish in Boston versus Topeka) and in individual preferences (e.g., bean lovers versus corn lovers) would be expected to vary, decisions at a national level will be inefficient. Were all jurisdictions to correspond to the extent of the externality, there would be no race to the bottom, because each jurisdiction would have an incentive to properly deal with pollution within its borders. That is, there might be greater variety in environmental outcome vis-à-vis uniform national standards, but that variety would provide citizens with great choice, being able to pick an inexpensive but dirty city or a more expensive but clean city.

V

EPILOGUE

There are two quite contrasting views of what the future will bring. The "Doomsters" believe that increasing worldwide income and population will result in ever-increasing use of materials and energy resulting in either a) resource depletion and economic or environmental collapse or b) ever-growing environmental pollution destroying ecosystems and human well-being. "Boomsters," on the other hand, believe that growing income will result in greater demand for environmental quality and natural resource preservation and that increased population will provide more minds and labor to solve problems as they emerge. Technological advances are viewed with suspicion by Doomsters who believe they bring heretofore unknown environmental problems, while technological advances tend to be embraced by Boomsters who argue that new technologies tend to be both cleaner and less resource intensive.

Both positions are extreme, hence likely to be incorrect. Doomsters are surely aware that some environmental problems have clearly diminished over time (e.g., U.S. air quality or the quality of the Thames River in England). And Boomsters have seen environmental disasters, such as aquifer damage at the Love Canal or the Times Beach dioxin episode, along with ongoing deterioration of certain environmental goods (e.g., the world's reefs and many fisheries). A better characterization of these positions is less extreme: Doomsters believe the future is going to be of a one-step-forward-two-steps-back nature, and Boomsters believe that the future will be of a two-steps-forward-one-step-back nature.

What will the actual future bring? Of course, one can never predict with accuracy what the future will bring. Indeed, accurate predictions would require unknowable information, for if we *really* could know in a meaningful way what the future would bring, we would not have to wait for it; we could have it now, if it were an improvement.

Whether the future will be better or worse depends greatly on decisions that are being made now and that will be made over the coming years. Even if many aspects of environmental quality are improving, that does not mean that they are improving at rates that are optimal. That is, we might in fact be in a two-steps-forward-for-each-step-backward world, when what we desire is a four-steps-forward-for-each-misstep world. It is clearly the case that environmental quality is a normal—and probably superior—good, hence one might expect that we would want our environmental portfolio to grow at least as rapidly as our financial portfolio. And the instances of *declining* environmental quality (e.g., the world's reefs, heavy metal buildup in the food chain) would seem to be clearly nonoptimal.

For two important reasons, one could argue that decisions made now and over the next seventy to one hundred years are going to be particularly critical for the future of our species as well as many other species that we care about. First, population is projected to continue growing over this period, reaching perhaps nine billion people (50% more people than at present) sometime in this century. After that time, population levels are projected to fall, resulting in reversals in the types of encroachment on nature that rising population has brought.[1] Second, there is great poverty at present in much of the world. To raise the welfare of the world's poor up to generally acceptable standards will be a daunting task, but one that is likely to take place over the coming century. Over certain ranges of income growth environmental pollution tends to increase before falling as nonindustrial output comes to dominate production in high income countries and as their demands for environmental quality grow.

The rises in population and income projected over the next century will present grave challenges. To meet those challenges, we will need, at a minimum, to make good decisions from the perspective of the economist. A view, implicit in much of this book, is that if we *really* made optimal decisions from our perspective as humans, we would be unlikely to do great damage to other species. This follows from the fact that we generally live in near proximity to our production facilities, so that the air we breathe and the water we drink affects us more than it does other species. Moreover, we want to give our offspring more than just financial wealth; we want our offspring to be able to live in a clean world, a world without significant loss of stocks of natural environmental resources. That is, if we economists did our job right, engaging in projects with accurately measured benefits to humanity greater than costs, we might have surprisingly few remaining environmental problems that would concern environmentalists.

It has been argued throughout this book, however, that we are not providing environmental quality at levels that are optimal for humans for a variety of reasons, some major and some minor. This leads to a number of recommendations for both economists and environmentalists with concerns for environmental quality or resource depletion. Some recommendations are quite general (e.g., joining environmental groups hoping to be perceived as the marginal voters needed to win the election, hence gaining more influence over environmental outcomes via the political process). Other examples would be the jurisdictional problems discussed in the previous chapter or the unrecognized fact that benefit-cost analysis for public goods is being conducted at the wrong income levels (as argued in chapter 8) and all of the ungenerated income would have been spent on the public good.

Other recommendations are much narrower, relating to the information that has been instrumental in legal and regulatory rulings regarding environmental quality. Many of those rulings have been based on faulty analysis. If damages can be perceived, the SSD approach will not do a good job of measuring the benefits of cleanup, because people will incur costs to avoid those damages. Moreover, if damages can be perceived, the property value hedonic results would need to be *added* to the wage value hedonic.

If damages cannot be perceived, the hedonic method will not do a good job of measuring the benefits of cleanup, because people will not pay for benefits they cannot perceive. In light of the fact that some categories of damage are perceived (e.g., smell or visibility) while other entirely different damage categories are not perceived, a case could be made for adding damages measured in both ways together. That this is so has never been seriously advanced in the policy arena, because the role of perceptions has not been deeply explored. For any specific policy, the relative weight of the arguments made in chapters 9 through 16 might vary, but in virtually all such cases, the arguments suggest undervaluation of environmental amenities.

Despite the many problems with benefit-cost analysis discussed throughout this book, this approach is still needed to prioritize the vast range of projects that are advanced by environmental economists and environmentalists. We must choose. If we choose well, there is reason for long-run optimism, hope for the human race and our environment.

NOTES

1. Most of the industrialized world is not currently replacing itself, which requires about 2.1 births per female. Only the United States is even close to that number, largely as a result of immigration, which is selective of the young in their childbearing years. Birthrates are plummeting even throughout the developing world, including Africa and Southeast Asia. At some point, it is likely that the population problem will be one of too few people, not too many people. Until that time, however, humans face many difficult choices.

Index

About the Author

Philip E. Graves, Ph.D., Northwestern University, 1973, is a professor whose interests currently lie in environmental economics, urban/regional economics, and applied price theory. His recent research emphasizes the role of labor supply market failures for optimal public goods provision and for the willingness-to-accept versus willingness-to-pay disparity. Similar issues of labor supply, as it varies according to whether technological progress occurs predominantly for new goods vis-à-vis existing goods, underlie Graves's recent work in economic growth and business cycles. He continues his long-standing interest in the role of amenities in the location and relocation decisions of households and in monetary economics, while pursuing several topics in applied microeconomics.